EARTH: The Toughest Boot Camp in the Universe

To my Texan
Friend
Lynda.
Love Isobel x
March 2017

Earth: The Toughest Boot Camp in the Universe by Elizabeth Taylor-Wey
Published by Australian eBook Publisher
www.AustralianEbookPublisher.com.au

1st Edition 2017, pbk.
ISBN: 978-1-925516-77-7

National Library of Australia Cataloguing-in-Publication entry:
Creator: Taylor-Wey, Elizabeth, author.
Title: Earth: The Toughest Boot Camp in the Universe / Elizabeth Taylor-Wey.
ISBN: 9781925516777 (paperback)
ISBN: 9781925516784 (epub)
ISBN: 9781925516791 (mobi)
Subjects: Psychology, Religious. Spirituality--Psychology.
Religious awakening. Spiritual life.

Also available as an ebook from major ebook vendors.

EARTH

The Toughest Boot Camp in the Universe

Elizabeth Taylor-Wey

I had the good fortune to meet Elizabeth Taylor-Wey during a training we attended at the Omega Institute New York with Dr Brian Weiss. She crossed the room to speak with me regarding past life regression therapy and how it would be of value in my medical practice. This conversation changed the course of my work, changed the course of my life and set me on a new direction.

She is a gifted healer and channel. Her work with the Guides and Spirits is magnificent. Elizabeth's gentle teaching and patience has been very helpful as she guides this Western doctor through uncharted waters. She has taught me everything about the work she does, and has encouraged my tentative steps into her world. She has always been there to support my work, my learning, my exploration, and as my teacher, she has gifted me with valuable critical review of the work that I have done so that I might see ways to improve. She has made me a better doctor, and she has helped me better help my patients. It is because of her support and encouragement that I have ventured out of the Western medical box into new vistas of integrative healing to my benefit and the benefit of those for whom I care. The course of my life would be altogether different had she not taken those steps and moved forward to say hello. I'm forever grateful for that handshake, and all the love and light that have followed.

Gil C. Grimes, MD
West Prince Family Health Clinic
Prince Edward Island. Canada.

Contents

Acknowledgements

This book is dedicated to my wonderful husband Dennis, who has always had absolute belief in me.

My heart is full of gratitude to my beautiful family, in particular Damien and Kylie, my wonderful friends, and Spiritual Guides who have been my inspiration. Your support and encouragement have been very important to the dedication and courage required to write this book. My gratitude and love to Donald James Waters OAM, the talented Australian contemporary artist responsible for this book's cover. Donald James Waters is an established Australian artist with an illustrious career spanning more than three decades and his career has taken his art to every corner of the globe. His distinctive style has made its way into the catalogues of many private and corporate collectors alike, including that of Her Majesty Queen Elizabeth II's art collection. This year (2016) Donald was awarded with an Order of Australia Medal (OAM) for services to the community and the Arts. To Paul and Melissa for your combined talents in photography and beauty. Thank you to Lindsay, my lifesaver during the process of editing. This book would not have been possible without my spectacular editor, Sylvia Marson of eagle eye editing, who exhibited extreme patience and support, a big thank you, for without your skills, I don't know how this book would have come together so beautifully.

Foreword

by Elizabeth Taylor-Wey

I am an Advanced Past Life Regression Practitioner, Master Teacher and Healer. Because of the gifts I have been blessed with, I have a strong and loving connection with the Spirit world. I understand through my Spiritual Guides, that there is a fine line between our Guides and us. Each of us is of equal importance and they only see the goodness in us as they guide us through our trials and tribulations. We are here to share love, kindness, compassion and light. When we do shine our light, we become ambassadors for peace on planet Earth. This is my life's work, to help people and to teach people, in the most loving, gentle ways possible; to guide those seeking emotional healing by understanding their life purpose. Your body is a miracle.

Within our Subconscious there is a phenomenal library of all there is to know, and it will do everything within its power to bring about a deeper understanding within you. The challenges throughout my life have given me a profound understanding of what matters, and while I admit my wisdom has come mostly from hindsight, I hope that this book will provide you with some assistance in avoiding those tangled roots of self-defeating thoughts, the ones that stop you from acknowledging your rightful place on planet Earth.

Warm hugs of friendship, love and light.

Elizabeth

Preface

Any book that imparts a knowledge of life,
is a good book.

Earth: The Toughest Boot Camp in the Universe has three parts. In Part 1, I reveal my story and the surprising events in my life, the revelations and my meetings with Spirits and Guides from the other side of the veil that have led me to where I am today. In Part 2, I share with you some of the incredible past life regressions I have had the privilege to facilitate. There are so many extraordinary stories that I could have written about in this book, however, over the years there have been past life experiences that have stood out for their uniqueness and, in my opinion, have demonstrated the diverse journeys the Soul can take, time after time. Part 3 contains chapters where I explore in more detail answers to some of the most important questions we have about life, and how to live a happy and fulfilled life. I connect with Guides and the Subconscious to further explore the meaning of our Soul's journey here on Earth and the impact on us of the lessons we are meant to learn in each lifetime.

You will be tested on your beliefs as some of the past lives will stretch your imagination to its limits. Revealing a past life and communicating with the Subconscious is like walking through a golden gateway of potentials and possibilities. It is a bold and fearless exploration into the fundamental core of your existence, one that will hopefully ignite a fire of hope and generate a deeper understanding of why you are here.

The phenomenal, all powerful Subconscious exists to champion your life journeys, it will never be drawn into exposing knowledge you are not ready to handle, nor will it disclose a confidence.

The purpose of the Subconscious is to provide positive guidance in helping you to achieve the challenges you set down for yourself; it is the master of the all-knowing higher aspect of ourselves.

The unique lives you experience are for you to learn from, and all deeds are written upon your Soul and these can be read as clearly as you might view your reflection in a mirror.

So, it is incumbent on you to build a solid foundation of unconditional love and non-judgement of yourself.

We have to believe in what feels right for us, to discover within ourselves a truth.

What may be your truth is not necessarily the truth of another.

We can only do our best, whatever that best is, and at the end of our life, just before we take our last breath, if we can look back and see we have learned our lessons, understood ourselves, been of value to humanity; then in my opinion, this is as fine a way to go as possible. So, as you strive for meaning in your lives, may truth be your light.

My hope is that this book finds a place in your heart, a place that resonates with your truth, and one that travels with you as you traverse your journey to this Earth, the toughest boot camp in the Universe.

Part 1
Boot Camp

"We all want to be special, to stand out and there's nothing wrong with this. The irony is that every human being is special to start with, because we're unique to start with.

But we then go through some sort of boot camp from the age of zero to about 18 where we learn everything we can about how not to be unique."

Karl Marlantes

Chapter 1
One Step at a Time

"That's one small step for a man, one giant leap for mankind."
Neil Armstrong

There comes a point in most of our lives when we wonder what it is all about. Struggles can seem endless, no matter who we are. The colour of our skin or our position in life has no bearing, at all; each of us must make and take the journey within. Understanding our strengths and weaknesses inevitably brings us to that point of recognising who we are, what we've done and what there is left to do. We get there eventually; however, it may be through many lifetimes. It is a comforting thought, knowing it will turn out all right in the end.

Fill yourself with the sparking light of love, and reach out and engage, and be fearless in your endeavours. Take a step back, open your heart and let go. This is so empowering, and you'll soon find that your energy creates a positive response in others, a reaction you may never have experienced before. Relinquish the need to always be right, have an open heart and allow the light of understanding to flow in.

Be more flexible, allowing yourself to become that loving caring person you were always meant to be.

At the end of experiencing a past life, the entity of that time is guided to the point just after death where they are asked for the purpose and lessons learned from the experiences of that particular life. The responses are always similar. Hindsight is a marvellous thing and it is something we have all wished we could have used to change a situation. The lessons are seen from a different perspective, one that is not judgemental. Each of us is learning to love, forgive and accept. To understand motives, to see how separation does not end relationships. All of these observations have an impact on us and will generally follow us until we have learned the lessons attached to a particular situation.

Imagine a filing cabinet filled to the brim with every single important event that has occurred on our Soul's journey; all this knowledge sits in the Subconscious.

It is not uncommon for someone who carries guilt to feel protective of themselves when they are going to experience a regression. We are all afraid of being judged by others, it is a real fear and comes from a deep-seated place.

You might think of it as a defence mechanism, one that has been acquired over many lifetimes of persecution.

These people are usually referred to as 'too sensitive', and they are always being told to toughen up.

If only they knew the full story, how it would change their lives and the lives of those around them. Regression is a powerful tool, thoughtfully inspiring people to challenge and celebrate their achievements by glancing into the past, to see experiences that may well change their current circumstances forever.

For those who might question the validity of this book, I'm hopeful that it may inspire you to become bolder and braver.

We spend our childhoods innocent of most things due to the natural flow of life, then adulthood finds us gaining strengths we could never have believed we would possess. You *will* have incredible stories inside of you, stories of tragedy, endurance, bravery and triumph. Stories of when you might have been a murderer, a cheat, a liar or a thief. By far the greatest revelation is in realising that race, culture, religion, gender and sexual orientation, have all been part of our many lives and if you have not experienced it yet, you will.

It is the only way by which the Soul can reach its final destination: back to the Source of love and light.

Each lifetime helps us to understand the roles we have taken on and the adventures we have had, no matter if we were the perpetrator or victim, successful, or otherwise.

By knowing that we experience these life lessons for the purpose of gaining wisdom, it becomes easier to be less judgmental and more compassionate towards each other.

Openly acknowledging that we *are* different, yet the same, allows us to be of greater value to each other.

The ultimate judge is our 'Soul'. It waits patiently for us to live out the life we chose, without interference, so that we can experience what it is that we came here to learn. When we have perfected our lessons, when we can honestly say we have never judged another, through anger or egoistical authority, then it is probably time we go home to the Light for good.

We will have served ourselves well.

Increasingly, the world's population is investing time, energy and money into seeking answers that will allow us to live the 'perfect life'.

We all play a role in this game called life, from Damascus to Dublin, Milan to Mexico, New York to the Netherlands, it does not matter, because there will always be a single key that belongs to you alone and when it is explored, you will find it unlocks a plethora of awareness, providing you with the opportunity to understand who you are, more than you could ever have imagined.

My dream has been to infuse others with a level of acceptance, to lift them to a heightened awareness of themselves and others, to inspire them to be illuminating and powerful, and to embrace every moment possible.

Chapter 2
My Story

"You can be the most beautiful person in the world and everybody sees light and rainbows when they look at you, but if you yourself do not know it, all of that doesn't even matter. Every second that you spend on doubting your worth, every moment that you use to criticise yourself; is a second of your life wasted, is a moment of your life thrown away. It is not like you have forever, so do not waste any of your seconds, do not throw even one of your moments away."

C. Joybell

It does not matter who we are, where we come from or what we may have done, what matters most is that we continue working towards self-improvement. When I was a little girl, I had a nightmare almost every night. The same horrible one, over and over and over, of falling out of a boat and sinking down into thick, slimy green water. Fighting for breath, I'd wake up screaming until my parents came in to soothe me back to sleep. Little did I know, I was experiencing a past life. Maybe it was the same reason I did not like being given gas at the dentist, or have ether dripped over a mask as an anaesthetic; if I close my eyes now, I can still remember those feelings of dread.

That lifetime was in the Mississippi; my family were known as swamp people. I had been arguing with my siblings, then gone down to where the wooden longboat was tied, looking to seek solace from the trouble I'd become embroiled in.

It seems my skills in using the boat were well known, but on this day as I pushed out with the long pole, anger was seething through me, and as I got deeper into the glades, I was not concentrating and the guiding pole became stuck.

I was thrown out of the boat and as I quickly sank into slimly green water, my neck became caught among some sticky roots, causing my sudden death.

Many years later, I came to understand that nightmare and was grateful, because since learning of this past life, I have totally lost the fear of drowning and suffocation. This lifetime was shown to me by my Spiritual Guide, Teloris.

My grandmother had a big influence on my life, and she lived in a small house next to our family home. She was a curious person and would often have a small group of friends visit her. I was always asking her about the big stone monastery she'd taken me to visit when I was younger, the one that had huge cauldrons of boiling water sitting on large stone blocks.

She would look at me as if I was crazy, nevertheless I was positive I'd been there.

I discovered much later in life that I had lived as a Monk in that monastery and my close friend in that life was my grandmother in this lifetime. I also learned she was a Spiritualist; today I have her diary, an old exercise book with a picture of the stunning Olivia De Havilland on the cover. My grandmother had titled it 'A Spiritualists Diary', and it was written before, during and after the Second World War.

Marjorie St John Savage, my grandmother, followed Rosicrucianism and was a member of this worldwide order claiming to possess esoteric wisdom handed down from ancient times.

They were seen as spiritual communities, seeking, studying and practising the metaphysical laws governing the Universe.

Her diary is a treasured recollection of those beliefs. It would be a long time before I learned how similar I was to my grandmother's ways in searching for answers from the Universe.

I grew up knowing I was a loner. I never fitted in with groups, only ever having the odd girlfriend or two. I disliked loud music, parties and boyfriends for that matter too. Do not get me wrong, I liked people, but I always seemed to know when they were not good people.

Fast-forward now to my early 20s when I began looking for answers, as I somehow knew there was something truly different about me. I could put my hands on old furniture and feel and see images of the previous owners.

After experiencing this, I wanted to know more and many of the Spiritual leaders were high on my list for investigation. I found myself liking their way of thinking. Far off in the world of Spirit, things for Elizabeth were beginning to stir ever so slowly. Lessons had to come first; for how could I give advice to another without any wisdom?

Life's experiences bring far greater wisdom than any learning from books.

Early into my 30s, I began to experience unique feelings, dreams of significance were becoming more prolific, and I was seeing and experiencing things I could not explain.

Sadly, my grandmother had passed on by then and there wasn't really anyone to speak with about these occurrences. I did, however, know one thing for certain, I was following a Spiritual path.

Over the course of 30-plus years, many events have unfolded; not when I wanted them to happen, but always in perfect Universal timing.

I have read many books by and/or studied under many of the greats—Dr Brian Weiss, Dolores Cannon, Marie Louise Von Franz, Carl Jung, and they gave me plenty of wisdom and allowed me to grow into the person I have become today.

However, it has been my Spiritual Guides who have been the greatest teachers. How have I reached this point?

THROUGH EXPERIENCE, FAITH AND a great amount of trust. I now realise that I had to go through all the challenges set before me, challenges far greater than I could ever have imagined. This book is about my final acceptance of the gifts given to me by Spirit and how I have used them to help fellow Soul travellers on their path to the freedom of body, mind and spirit.

How did my Spirit Guides finally get my attention?

With a huge concrete demolition ball swung against my stubborn head, that's how! Oh, how I wished my Grandmother had still been alive.

Chapter 3
The Gift

"God prepares leaders with a specific place and task in mind. Training methods are adapted to the mission, and natural and spiritual gifts are given with clear purpose."
J Oswald Sanders

In a matter of hours my life would change forever. I did not know what that something would be, or what sort of effects a long-awaited appointment would have on me, but nothing could have possibly prepared me for what was to eventuate.

Would I have run in the opposite direction?

Possibly not, as I have always stepped into where no man fears to tread; but mind you, this was to be a little out of the ordinary.

Hearing a message from the Spirit world is a life-changing experience, and I was preparing myself for this with great excitement. After all, I had been shortlisted for almost 18 months. Simone was famous, the best of the best. I'd been to see her years earlier, and all of her previous predictions were accurate and if they hadn't happened already, they were sure to come true down the track.

By this time I was 36, and wanted to spend the rest of my life focusing on a purpose, one that would develop a stronger foundation for who I wanted to become.

I spent the early morning dressing with care, everything felt calm and perfect and I didn't want anything to disrupt my preparations. Life had drawn many difficulties into my corner and by the end of that long wait, I was more than ready to see Simone.

Breaking away from the situations I had found myself in was uppermost in my mind. I wanted peace and freedom. I'd be lying if I said my nervousness didn't equal my excitement. My questions had built up over several weeks of reflection and I wanted to tackle the hard bits. It was almost as if I was subconsciously pushing out the old to make room for the unknown.

SIMONE HAD A SHELL and a stone, and I was to take along photos of people, both alive and dead, to which she would place under the appropriate item. Shell for life, stone for death.

People say that knowledge is power, the more knowledge the more power and they would be right if they'd been in my shoes four months on from this particular date with destiny. I'd arrived early and was sitting with my thoughts, watching Simone and her client deep in discussion.

The garden surroundings were beautiful in a crazy, wild unkept way, with splashes of hot pink and orange bougainvillea, and delicate tendrils of purple wisteria made their own bold statements by climbing over anything that gave support to their long flowering tendrils.

Life hadn't been easy for me and, more often than not, the lessons had been of my own creation. I attempted to focus on the beauty around me, but instead I started crying.

My heart was aching, and I'd like to have thought I was going to handle that day like I did on my last visit to Simone, but for me the traumas I had been through since then seemed to be taking control of me.

The world can seem so cruel at times, and there seemed to be no formula to protect myself from pain. Yet there are people who go through life, who by some good fortune, never appear to have such dramas. An appealing thought. It is only through pain and heartache that I am about to understand the true meaning of compassion, and through my faults learn humility.

My wonderful family has watched me be many times a pathetically wretched and fallen Soul. They have watched me fight my way out of deep, multiple depressions, with countless amounts of tears. They have forgiven me more times than I care to remember.

The list of mistakes could go on forever, nevertheless soon enough I will be grateful for those mistakes and for the journey I was about to embark on.

The unseen world of Spirit *never* gives up on us, no matter what.

Preoccupied with my thoughts, I almost did not hear my name being called. My stomach did a somersault, lurching awkwardly like some trapeze artist, slipping then fighting to gain balance.

I WISH IT WERE easier to put my emotions into words, to describe the feelings that are stirring in my heart regarding this story I'm about to write. It may read to you as unbelievable, but every word is true.

I may not have believed the story myself and probably would have said as much before this traumatic experience was to unfold, one that would change my life forever.

"JUST A MOMENT ELIZABETH," Simone called out, "I'll be back shortly." She walked towards the side of the house.

She returned a few minutes later, chatting away to herself, or so I thought, until I saw her looking down and chatting to a Butcher bird, walking by her side. As she beckoned me over, that bird walked up to me and looked up and deep into my eyes for what seemed ages, before simply taking off and flying away.

I mentioned to Simone that I thought it a little weird and she simply smiled.

The reading began.

She predicted my son would be in Morocco climbing a snow-covered mountain in the next few days. True. She would tell me that my father, who'd already passed over, was in the kitchen the day my grandson and husband were wearing Christmas hats and preparing Christmas lunch. True.

The reading came to an end and Simone would not take payment. In fact, she said she had a gift for me, while also assuring me that I didn't have to accept it. But I admired her greatly and I was in a vulnerable state, so willingly accepted her generosity.

Off she went and came back with a small stone in her hand; it was smooth and reminded me of a small, round shaped coin purse.

It is known on many native islands around the world that leaving the land as you found it shows great respect for these most beautiful, spiritual places. People who take rocks from sacred sites can be sure of trouble, even if it is gifted to you by another. I was unaware of this and would never in a million years have accepted the gift if I had known.

Although, I guess, Spirit would have kept trying, whatever it took. On the way home I decided to call in on my daughter and show her the stone.

I was exhausted but excited, my head spinning as I was coming to realise something important was happening, along with a sense that it was not going to slow down.

At this point in my life I didn't claim to know much on the subject of spirituality, other than that I loved it and I had begun practising a few psychic readings years before.

Although all of our stories are different, it is my hope that those of you with a curious mind will find comfort from the journey I'm about to share with you. Know that anything and everything is possible in the world of Spirit.

There was still so much healing to be done on the inside for me, although I do not know this yet.

I still needed to grow up and learn that there was much more to life than my own bubble of comfort and happiness. It will become necessary for me to experience the world, the suffering, the pain and the joy so that I could understand the future role I had been chosen to play.

At this point in time, though, I was completely unaware, to which I can assure you was a blessing in disguise.

I carefully placed the stone in my daughter's hand, telling her that it was a gift from Simone. Immediately she began to dance and sway, telling me she felt as light as a feather, but just as suddenly she puts the stone back into my hand telling me it is not for her to hold.

That was ok with me anyway, I needed to go home and rest.

Later that evening as I prepared for bed, I put the stone on my bedside table. Sleep came fast and then just as quickly it became eerie. I woke up to my right arm stretching out, allowing my hand to hold the stone. I had no control over that action.

My hand took the stone to my heart and held it there for a few minutes, then just as carefully the hand took the stone and placed it back on the bedside table. It was at that precise moment that the real journey began.

My hand investigated every part of my body, every crevice, every single part of everything, and from that point on, I was, as the saying goes, possessed.

Yes, indeed, possessed.

Immediately, I was able to do everything that was possible in terms of clairvoyance and psychic readings and mediumship.

Automatic writing, retrieving past lives in the blink of an eye, sitting with anybody and everybody and telling them things about themselves they had forgotten, where they lived when they were young, even to describing the precise details of the interior of the home they had lived in, who they were related to, what they ate, describing the reasons for scars on their bodies, pretty much everything about their lives.

The flow of information was constant and was identified in every case as correct to the minutest detail.

The following Sunday morning I was reading the newspaper, when my hand went across to pick up a pen. Moving back to the page the pen began circling the photo of a young girl who had gone missing from a train station some weeks earlier, it circled many times around this photo and then it began to write.

The words flowed, as the energy attached to me described the whole experience of this child's death. It drew an image of the abductor, the type of vehicle he drove, where he had taken the child, what he had done to her. It was so shocking, I felt I had no choice but to go to the police.

Not just any police station mind you, but Headquarters in the city. Thank goodness for my innocence, because if I had known what I would be going through that day I would not have left the kitchen table.

In the meantime, all I could focus on was a positive outcome for the parents, anything that might help them find their daughter.

The police led me to the tactical room where detailed maps of an area the child was thought to be in lay open, indicating large dark green images of bushland, highlighted with lines of blue and red, marking locations of water and roads.

I was nervous, my clothes were feeling uncomfortable in the heightened chill of the air-conditioned room, and I was alert to the fact that my physical body's reaction had my shirt clinging to the small of my back.

I hoped that my head would be as clear as it had been from the initial understanding of this whole messy matter, so I was still brimming with anticipation towards the task at hand and could not allow myself the luxury of believing this would not happen.

There seemed to be a stubborn resistance from the entity to help me, and I felt my courage slipping away and turning to fear as I realised I would not be pinpointing any spot that morning and was led red-faced to the front door. I stood on the footpath rubbing my temples; this cannot be happening, surely the information I had been given was right? It was eleven o'clock and I was too tired to think straight.

The journey home passed in a flash. My head was full of jumbled images of a body buried in a shallow grave near water, to a murderer laughing at not being caught out, but also of the face of that little girl, so innocent.

I could not let go.

Later that day, the entity upped the anti because as I lay down to rest so did the images return, a voice telling me more and more about this sexual predator, this time with an exceptional amount of information, and I was again shown the place where the body was.

I was shown how the little girl was sexually abused and how she was murdered, where the perpetrator lived and what colour his car was. I decided to go and find out for myself.

A good friend, who I'd confided in, insisted on coming with me. I'm sure she believed I was losing my mind. The sun was riding high by the time we reached the area I had been guided to, and as we drove into a particular street, my arm shot out of its own accord and pointed to a house, the exact one that had been described to me earlier the day before. The hairs went up on my arms and a chill ran through my body. I was thinking at the same time, what the heck do I do about this now? My friend suggested we should drive home and think about it a little more, and after a two-hour drive I had determined I would need to go back to the police. Like a trapdoor opening, I dropped down into yet another crazy maze. I did contact the police, and this time I met up with them and led them through the bush. But again, this entity let me down, and I was asked not to call the police again.

Can't say I blamed them.

The communication with this entity did not abate; it guided me to the phone book and pointed out a specific number, telling me that it belonged to relative of the missing child. It further informed me that on a sideboard in this relative's house was a photo of the girl and her aunt playing softball.

I made the call and sure enough the person on the end of the line was a relative, but not with the same surname as the child, so I was really shocked, particularly after I mentioned the softball photo and the phone slammed down.

It was becoming very difficult for me, my personality was changing and I could not do a thing about it. Remember, at this stage I did not know I was possessed. So many things happened and at such a fast pace; life was extreme.

Very early one morning, I became frustrated, nervous, bewildered and most of all frightened by the last of what I would call horrifying experiences.

Yet I felt I had no choice but to continue because this entity told me the murderer knew my name and was at the end of my street, sitting in a red car. My heart pounded and my hands shook as the negative thoughts feeding my fear crawled over me.

I got up quickly and raced into the bedroom to try and stop my husband from taking his morning walk. He was not impressed.

I phoned a police friend, he had just arrived home from a night shift and wasn't happy with my call, but dear soul that he was, he made the effort and came over. Unknown to me, my husband and friend had decided I needed to see a doctor.

When Steven arrived I told him about the car, and after calming down my insane panic attack, he agreed to drive down to the end of the street.

I had to push all thoughts of fear from my mind, and to keep thinking everything was going to be all right.

But then Steven saw the red car, and immediately he was on the phone asking for information on the registration; how he continued to be so calm and logical was beyond me, but then he was a policeman. He discovered that the car belonged to a man living locally, so then I was back to square one. Steven, however, was unimpressed and left soon after.

Thank goodness my husband had also left for work, allowing me time to collect my thoughts and settle my nerves. I felt wretched, would this entity ever leave me alone?

The following day, my husband told me that there was someone who could help me. As soon as the entity knew this, it began to apologise for everything it had done to me and wanted to be able to speak with the person as soon as they arrived.

It was around lunchtime the next day that Jenny arrived. I began explaining that this entity wished to speak to her, but she was not interested, and without further ado she asked me to sit down.

Taking my hands, I was asked to imagine white light, something I had never heard of before.

Before my eyes I saw a wave of energy moving, continually back and forth, through my arm. Jenny was saying that I needed to let it go, believe me I was trying, then without warning it was gone. It felt as though I had just come out of a coma, it left me feeling strangely empty. For all those months I could see, feel and experience anything I wanted to, do anything I wanted to and in less than a minute it had disappeared.

The one thing I had wanted most that whole time was to feel normal again.

But that was never going to happen, because the real part of my spiritual journey was just beginning.

I learned later that the entity was a pilot that had died in a chopper crash; he realised he could manipulate me and was very remorseful in the end. I was happy for him that he had gone to the Light.

This was the same day I learned of a Guide named Teloris.

Chapter 4
Teloris

"To see the universal and all-pervading Spirit of Truth face to face, one must be able to love the meanest of all creation as oneself."
Mahatma Gandhi

How does one describe the word *love* when explaining a depth of feeling for someone? How does one express the feeling of pure energy felt when looking deep into their eyes, eyes that seem to be aware of everything about you?

My thoughts rocked backwards and forwards as I registered in my mind just what I was experiencing.

Destiny had willed this moment.

Instead of my old world, a new one would emerge, overriding everything I'd ever encountered previously in my life.

But who could I trust to tell this story to, who would believe my story?

It was early morning and a vision beyond Earthly explanation appeared in front of my eyes. The veil between Spirit and Elizabeth was lifted.

My body seemed curiously non-existent as I felt myself standing at the end of a long table with no obvious supporting legs, it was floating as if in mid-air, way beyond our Earthly understanding.

At the end of the table was a beautiful woman, her hair drawn back, her face beaming with unconditional love and peace. For the first time in my life, I experienced 'real' love.

A peace beyond explanation, a love so tender I thought my heart would burst, an indescribable radiance of love was streaming from her energy, permeating the air between us.

Although there existed nothing but complete silence, it was as if there was no room for anything other than the thought of being filled with infinite love, understanding, patience, kindness, gentleness and extraordinary wisdom.

After my initial awareness, this divine presence signalled me to move to another table. I thought I could hear other voices, low and close by, whispering as if they were trying to include me in their conversation. I caught a glimpse of them, it felt strange, but safe. In the middle of this table sat a sphere that appeared to be carved from timber, forming a lacy open-work ball.

Inside was a beautiful white dove.

I felt as though I belonged at this table.

It would be years later before I would be back there again.

I opened my eyes to my bedroom and shook my head, unnerved by the strength of my emotions.

The world that had existed a few hours earlier in the quiet of my home had disappeared beneath the sweeping experience I had just encountered. The sense that someone was looking over me, caring for me with such deep unconditional love, love that was so powerful, it seemed almost as if a frontier between past lives and present life was merging as one, it was and it did. I closed my eyes again, attempting to recapture those incredible emotions and they were still there. I bounced out of bed with the excitement of someone who had just been given a new lease on life; injected with pure happiness, there was a subtle awareness of skills as a healer and a wise woman coming to life.

There would be a few unsettling human emotions of spirit and body to experience before I could assist to heal. I have since been taught about the ancient wisdom of healing, drawing from my Guides the support needed to keep going with trust and faith.

A few days later I was introduced to a Spiritual practitioner called Yolanda.

She told me the beautiful woman I had seen was my grandmother, and went as far as to leave the room and return soon after to place a smaller version of the carving I had told her about into my hands.

Yolanda asked me to join a spiritual circle, explaining that normally I would have to do training, but that she would make an exception for me. I told her I appreciated her invitation but that sort of thing was not for me.

Not long after that meeting, Yolanda passed away. It would be some years later before I'd meet her daughter Jenny, only to have the same invitation offered to me. This time I would accept.

Recovering from the sacred stone saga, my life's journey connected like dots on a map, guiding me to a higher calling. There was no doubt I had experienced a mammoth Spiritual awakening of undeniable proportions and my outlook on life had become more accepting.

I was no longer skeptical, but openly optimistic and trusting.

I was warmly received into Jenny's home, and I found myself engaging with a small, loving group of people, each of whom were there to support each other on their Spiritual journey. This awakening did not come for me straightaway, however, there was lots of work ahead. Learning to meditate, learning to ground with white light, learning to trust and have faith, and time after time these lessons were tested. Now, let me tell you, I'm a creative person and I have a pretty good imagination, but nothing could have prepared me for what was to come next.

Have you ever had a moment in your life where a thought was not your own? Have you ever felt an urge to do something out of character without knowing why?

One day, Jenny told us as we sat in our circle, that she would guide us back to a past life, and give us gentle direction as to what to do once there. She then took us through the steps to ground in the white light of protection, which allowed us to be guided safely through meditation into a past life. We listened carefully as Jenny told us to be open-minded to whatever we became aware of, either words or images, that would reflect a life we had lived. She directed us each step of the way, and although we could hear her words, we were able to see and hear images and conversations in our minds. Well, that is what I believed the others were also experiencing. Nevertheless, for me, that is exactly what happened, even though I can assure you, I was more than skeptical. The honest truth be known, it takes far less courage to believe in past life experiences than you may think.

It is so rewarding, finding the round peg that fits into the perfect round hole, and understanding that your life does have meaning. My understanding of my relationship with Teloris was to come through experiencing this past life.

We were Māori and lived hundreds of years ago.

It seemed to take forever, but eventually Jenny was asking for me to look down at my feet; they were small and brown.

I looked at my body, it was of a young female child, I would say about 8 years old with long dark-brown hair. She was wearing a hessian-type of fabric, her skin was a deep shade of copper brown. Was I really seeing this? Why did it feel so real?

I observed a deep valley flanked by two huge mountain sides covered in rich green foliage, massive trees of gigantic proportions and a path leading down one side into the valley.

I burst out crying, because through every fibre of my body I knew I had come home. I did not understand, how this could feel so real? I cried so hard until I was crying buckets of tears.

I heard Jenny's voice saying you can just observe you do not need to be attached; but the pull was so great, it was too late, I was home and that was that. Jenny was telling me to listen for my spiritual name, personally I thought that was going a bit too far and that there would be no way I would hear anything; when out of the blue I heard 'Tamara, Tamara'.

It was so real.

I followed a path which led me to the edge of a clearing. I saw elderly Māori women sitting around a fire, and there in all her glory was my grandmother, Teloris. I was guided to see where I slept, to see a happy time, and a sad time; I was shocked that those images could still have remained within me.

I realised that Teloris and I were herb gatherers and healers; I could see clearly her teaching me the making of remedies from plants and bark and, most importantly, how to heal through touch. It was just like watching a home movie and towards the end when I saw that Teloris had died, I was beyond grief. What that experience taught me was that all the lives we live are so intricately connected, and the knowing that we are never deserted by those that love us.

Experiencing my past life with Teloris gave me answers and changed my life forever by allowing my relationship with myself to become stronger and more dynamic than anything I had ever known before. To face my fears, to trust her in every area of my life, and to turn to her and away from things I had become used to. I was no longer living the life I had always been familiar with, where I stumbled along unaware of anything but myself; this was a huge step, as comfort zones were stripped away to allow me to live a more purposeful life. Slowly but surely, there was a joy filling my Soul, my spirit was being renewed, I felt truly on the path to victory over all that had affected me for so long.

Do not let me deceive you into thinking it was easy; in fact, it was an extremely difficult path I had chosen and would become an even harder journey to take.

Chapter 5
Amon

"All is within yourself. Know your most inward self and look for what corresponds with it in nature."
Ancient Egyptian Proverb

During this same period of time, I visited a medium who was to tell me of a lifetime I'd had in Egypt. As she laid her hands on me I saw a sequence of events unfold.

It appeared that I was a young boy who was about 10 years old, and I was watching myself working in a courtyard from which wide stone steps led up and into the private sanctuaries of four different temples. I saw that my task was to keep the red sandy courtyard clear of debris, and I believe I lived and slept in one corner of the court. I heard a priest calling to me, I was afraid and wondered if I'd done something wrong. But that was not the case, he was asking if I would like to learn to read and write. He was what one might call a maverick, an unorthodox, very independent-minded priest who was not liked at all by his fellow associates. His rooms were down under the main floor of the temple, and the walls and floor were laid with a large stone-type material.

By the light of oil lamps, I noticed that the walls held shelves holding hundreds of beautifully rolled scrolls, wrapped in a soft gold fabric, and they appeared utterly magical to my mind.

I realised that most of the scrolls had been written by myself. Over many years my master had taught me everything he knew about the occult, and I saw that it was knowledge far from acceptable to the other Priests. The images moved me to a time where I looked to be about 18 years of age, and I watched on as a

Priest came to our room, a representative on behalf of the other Priests. My dear old friend was being summoned. I begged him not to go, as I had a bad feeling. I heard him putting my mind at ease and off he went. I would never see him again for he was murdered for not revealing his Spiritual secrets.

These images went on and on and I imagined it being similar to that old adage about life passing before your eyes. I moved to a scene that appeared to be some years later, and those same priests were coming to that same room I'd continued living and studying in. I saw myself being asked to hand over the same secrets that my old friend had refused to do so long ago. Suddenly a priest lunged forward and slammed a poisoned spike into my chest. I fell to the floor, writhing in agony until I died.

I could hear a priest ask what should be done with my body; throw it to the dogs another said.

This is how I saw my body, lying on a rubbish heap being eaten by wild dogs. My Soul was very disturbed and it appeared that a fragment of my Soul still lingered in that horrific time.

It was healed on the day I saw this whole remarkable life.

Did I have doubts?

It was hard to have any, because I observed it so vividly.

Four years later I was in Sydney visiting my old friend, Neil.

A man with whom I have worked alongside throughout many a lifetime. The amazingly talented Neil was providing me with a healing, when out of the blue he told me I would soon have a new Guide. I asked for a name and was told quite clearly that he would introduce himself when he was ready.

Early one morning, a few months later, as I was in meditation on a completely different subject, I heard a booming voice say:

"God Bless you Child, my name is Amon and I am your Guide."

First of all, I was in shock, for where was my beloved Teloris?

He told me that her work had been done, but I was not going to have a bit of this, no, no, I was not! This beautiful Guide for whom I had this deep unconditional love for was not going anywhere. I just would not accept that for a second, so it was agreed that she would stay close by, albeit in the background.

We still communicate from time to time.

My love for her will never falter. I'm digressing a wee bit here, but for those of you who have a loving Guide, you know how wonderful it is to have such a loving support in your life.

So, there I was, sitting in my meditation chair, listening to Amon when all of a sudden like a lightning bolt, a thought struck me. I asked Amon if he had been my teacher in the lifetime I'd had in Egypt. Amon acknowledged himself as my old teacher and although now a little less in the flesh than before, he is still one of my spiritual advisors, 4000 years later.

Now that is amazing in anyone's eyes.

Do you believe this story?

It does not matter to me, because I know it to be the absolute truth in every detail.

Chapter 6

Archangel Raziel—Master Guide. Keeper of Secrets—Angel of Mysteries

"Archangel Raziel is the keeper of the Divine secrets of God. He reveals holy secrets when God gives him permission to do so."
Elizabeth Taylor-Wey

We *think* we know it all.

The next leg of my journey is one I know, for sure, that you, the reader, will be spellbound by.

The Spirit world would send signals to me that were all too clear, and in such a way that I would know these experiences to be extraordinary. Here I will relate the circumstances surrounding Archangel Raziel coming into my life. I will show you how spiritual awareness comes hand-in-hand with trust and faith. I am certain Lorna Byrne, the wonderful communicator with Angels, who wrote the spellbinding book *Angels in My Hair*, would attest to this.

This first-hand account reflects unconditional love, intrigue, trust and the incredible way in which the Universe worked with such magnificent timing to bring five Souls back together in this lifetime. Thank goodness there are others who can attest to this amazing experience.

The ball started rolling with a simple catch-up.

I have a dear friend who I call 'Your Royal Highness' as she has the name of a Queen. We became firm friends after realising we shared a similar curiosity for the metaphysical.

As strangers, we'd embarked on a unique spiritual course, and after having supported each other through the rigours of that training, this beautiful friendship was cemented and has remained that way ever since. Victoria is an authority on Astrology and Tarot. She had been living in Melbourne when I first met her and, much to my joy, later moved to Brisbane. One day we decided to meet for coffee, and we talked about a zillion things. Victoria mentioned a healer by the name of Ron Wilding. She told me that Ron could heal people when they were not present, that he practised what is known as absent or remote healing; a method in which the healer and the patient can be great distances away from each other.

My ears pricked up as she went on to say that Ron was directed by his Spirit Guides, that he 'sees' his way through the patient's body, patching wounds and painful areas with healing gels, tape and gauze, things the untrained eye cannot see.

I was excited, there was someone else doing what I did, but in a vastly different manner.

I needed to meet this man.

Little did I know our meeting was to come about in the most unexpected of ways. Victoria gave me Ron's phone number and soon after I arrived back home I was on the phone asking if I could come to meet him as soon as possible.

The voice at the other end was not so eager to engage in conversation and told me quite abruptly that not only did he no longer teach but that he didn't have time to meet people anymore. I was so disappointed, because for some reason I felt in my heart we would meet.

One Saturday morning a few weeks later, my husband and I were watching our grandsons playing a game of soccer, when my phone rang. The same gruff voice said that if I wished to see him I could go that morning. I replied that I was on my way, and to get there on time meant leaving immediately for a two-hour drive.

What was this powerful pull?

I did arrive on time and waiting to greet me was an elderly gentleman, wearing slippers and a grey cardigan; not that I knew what to expect, but this was certainly a surprise. After a tour though Ron's delightful garden, we went inside only to hear that familiar ring of a Skype phone call. It was a man in America, worried about his mother's health. Excusing himself, Ron set to work describing in accurate detail the current health of this woman.

The man on the screen was mindblown, as was I, as the information Ron gave was so accurate.

In the middle of this distant healing, there was a knock at the door. I went to answer it and there before me was one of the prettiest faces I had ever seen. I apologised for answering the door, explaining that Ron was busy. She introduced herself as Helena, and explained that she had brought Ron a homemade chicken curry for his lunch.

The Universe was at it again.

Together we sat quietly, waiting for Ron to finish the call.

Soon after, he walked across to greet Helena with a warm embrace, then took his place on a comfortable chair to resume our conversation. Raising his voice, Ron asked me how I would heal lungs that were full of fluid. I started to give my answer when he interrupted me by saying, "No, no, no, this is what you should do!"

I felt so embarrassed and said I should leave. Nonsense, Ron and Helena said simultaneously, stay for lunch.

There is no shortcut to this story, and you will soon understand the ways in which the Spirit world can work. I remember that delicious chicken curry and salad meal and the vibrant conversations so clearly as if it was yesterday. We sat at a small dining table, the meal we shared was obviously meant for two and I appreciated the generosity. I realised that teachers come is all kinds of packages.

Ron nodded to Helena through the meal and told her I would do as a healer and I felt as though I had been blessed by the Pope.

'Let's do lunch' took on a whole new meaning.

Thanking these beautiful people profusely for their generosity, I headed home with a whole lot to think about. The following Monday I received a call from Helena. She asked me if I had felt anything when I had put my hand on her arm. I thought back, but no, I could not remember. It was the complete opposite for her, she'd felt, what I now know to be, the familiar feeling of 'healing energy'. It reminded me of something my husband had said some years earlier, 'you should not put your hand on people, it has a funny effect'. An invisible thread was bringing five people together in a union of light and knowledge.

Even if one tried to bring an experience like this to actualisation, it could never be as seamless as the way the Universe orchestrated this so magnificently. Tick tock, tick tock, the unflappable clock of divine timing was rolling over to the moment in which a contractual agreement was to be honoured. The past and future were about to collide. A brief moment in time would change five people's lives forever. Helena told me that for weeks the Angel cards she used were indicating that a particular teacher would appear in her life.

In the short time that we met she knew that I could help guide her as a teacher though particular aspects of her life, things that were important for her spiritual growth. I also felt as though I was there to teach her, so I decided to invite Helena for a visit.

At the same time, for some unexplainable reason, I invited three other people I knew.

I was going to teach them how to channel past lives through the laying on of hands. Victoria and Amanda would only need to come a short distance, Neil from Sydney and Helena from the Sunshine Coast.

It was the middle of winter and a chilly front had swept over, bringing cold temperatures and strong winds, so I built a fire to bring warmth and atmosphere to the room.

One by one my friends arrived, Helena being the last.

It was only later that she told me how she had felt when she walked through the front door, describing to me the potent energy filling the living room, a presence of something powerful. I honestly had no idea why I felt inclined to bring these Souls together, after all it was only Helena who had asked to see me.

Everyone was polite and I daresay a little non-plussed at what would happen, perhaps even a little nervous about what they could or could not do.

There was a healing table set up ready to go.

I stood to one side instructing them on how to see a past life by placing their hands on a body. At one point there were three people with their hands on Helena, with all three seeing the same life.

Without preconceived notions, it is interesting to see how innocence can work in favour of the pupil.

Time after time I have seen this in my teaching practice.

However, things were not as they seemed. I had this great urge to step forward and place my hands on Helena and it was from that point that the words flowed from my mouth. As much as this may seem a fabricated tale, I can assure you categorically that I had never heard of Archangel Raziel, and I mispronounced his name initially.

"God Bless you children, my name is Archangel Raziel and I am the Master Guide for dear Elizabeth."

"Finally we have the Chosen Five together and hasn't it been a task and a half. I congratulate you Elizabeth on following your instincts; of course it was I directing you, but it would not have happened without your determination."

"I shall now speak to each of you."

And so it was that Archangel Raziel spoke, and there were messages of encouragement for each of us on the paths we had chosen to take.

He told us friendships would be tested and that we must carry on, come what may.

That it was inevitable that we would go down this path to learn what lay ahead, and the only way of avoiding it was by deciding not to take that path at all.

My eyes had been closed throughout the channel and when I felt that there was no more, I opened my eyes to look at the others. I knew instinctively that in a magnificent act of spiritual connection, Archangel Raziel had brought the five of us out of the shadows and into the light. As you can well imagine, the rest of the day took on a different meaning, one that was both exciting and extraordinary. We spoke for a long time that day and before everyone left for home, they had extracted a promise from me to seek answers from Archangel Raziel about the life we had shared together. What we did not realise was that this experience was appropriate and fitting to our purpose in this life. Within the context of time and over many lifetimes it appeared that the one we share now is a continuation of a specific contract.

It will take a whole lot of tough decisions from each of us, especially me, just to get up enough courage to believe in myself enough.

Let alone try and channel an Archangel I never knew existed in the first place!

Chapter 7

The Chosen Five: Elizabeth–Victoria–Amanda–Neil–Helena

"It isn't until you come to a spiritual understanding of who you are—not necessarily a religious feeling, but deep down, the spirit within—that you can begin to take control."

Oprah Winfrey

Spiritual experiences are, without exception, overwhelming. You become conscious of something far more powerful than you could imagine; a heightened intensity rises within you that is almost impossible to describe. The feeling is warm and loving, filling you with overwhelming inner peace and happiness.

I will experience this force of goodness and awe-inspiring energy as Archangel Raziel and I have our first private conversation. I had promised my friends that I would seek clarification of the life we had shared, and so the next day I set out to explore the possibility of another connection with the phenomenal Spiritual world. The following story is, word for word, the communication with a mighty Archangel. Much like a baby taking its first tentative steps, I was a little unsure of how to connect.

I thought to ground myself in white light and as I did, Archangel Raziel's loving energy washed over and through me, as it had done the day before.

It felt like a wave of intense heat flowing through every cell of my being, as the words flowed out through my voice box.

"Elspeth, you are to be commended on the way in which you followed your instincts. It is not easy to begin with and we understand that all sorts of questions have been raised, least of all the question on the authenticity of it all.

Be left in no doubt, my dear, that the messages you brought through were accurate. I will explain why we have brought the five of you together, and it is only when I have finished my words to you, that this journey will begin in earnest. It will be through dedication to your individual abilities, gifts as you might like to think of them, that this commitment will be successful."

This magnificent messenger of the Divine continued on.

"Welcome, children, welcome, I am Archangel Raziel. I have been responsible for many of the spiritual understandings that each of you have stored deep within your Soul memory, and this moment is the culmination of many centuries of planning.

Even if you do not believe to begin with, I hope that after much contemplation you will come to find the truth that lies between the words I will impart to you. I have said that each of you have a valuable gift and so I will tell you of a particular lifetime you shared together before clarifying each of your gifts.

Many hundreds of years ago in the year 1701, the five of you lived together at Elderberry Farm not far from a small village in Wisconsin. You were Druids, born from families who had taught you their secrets.

There is one amongst you who has led many lifetimes as a teacher in all things spiritual, and that one is Elspeth.

Training for her in this way came from and over many thousands of years. Elspeth, these dear Souls have always been your pupils, although certainly not always as novices, for indeed they are truly magnificent spiritual beings in their own right. The reason that we call you Chosen Ones in this lifetime is that it is in this time that each of you have the most to teach and give to others."

Archangel Raziel's voice was radiating such love, and he turned his thoughts to speak of Helena.

"We will begin with you, dearest Helena. We are pleased to welcome you back to this very special group. I hope that you have the courage and belief to continue.

Your name was May and you were the youngest.

At 15 years of age you were a keen pupil.

You spent years studying many of the ailments people suffered from, using herbs, bark, grasses and liquids made from a sea animal known as a squid, the squid ink being a basis for many of your concoctions. As was the way in those days, you had other duties and obligations that revolved around your group of friends, meaning the other four.

You were being groomed to become a healer and sought many ideas from those same friends. It was not easy for you Helena, for there was no time to play, so to speak; you always wore a yellow ribbon in your hair because it reminded you of the joy of life itself. You felt compelled to be knowledgeable in the understanding of the human form and would have no trouble dissecting an animal body that had recently passed over. You might ask, why has this taken so long, but the fact was, you had a number of Karmic lessons to experience and finally they are over and you can move forward.

This will be your last Earthly lifetime, my old friend, and you must use your time now to help as many others as possible to understand themselves and move forward in their lives.

You will one day become a Wise Counsel, or a Spirit Guide as you like to call us over here, or just here really.

We are very close to you all and do not see ourselves as anything but a mere separation of the spirit veil.

Now to your part in this beautiful group of Chosen Souls.

Understand that you play a pivotal role in this group, I cannot stress strongly enough the impact of your responsibility and so it is as follows.

We ask you to continue on the singular path you are travelling but that if you are asked for advice it is your job to help immediately. Three times a year you will meet with the others to speak of improvements and dreams that we will be sending to you with what we want you to say and do. In a few years' time or even less you will hold, along with others, seminars in many different places of your country."

Archangel Raziel then spoke of Neil. My body felt different, now strong and powerful. The voice coming from me was very deep, warm and profoundly loving.

"Now to my dear old friend Neil, known as Thomas, welcome to you, it is so good to be communicating with you after so many hundreds of years; you and I have been connected since the beginning of time. Yes, we were all from Atlantis.

You and I were teachers together in Atlantis, we were responsible for gathering information on huge computers, much more sophisticated than the ones you have in your society today.

On our computers we recorded the histories and mysteries of the Universes. There will be many who argue that Atlantis did not exist, but I can assure you Neil, that it did and still does.

It has been a very long time since I spoke of this place for it has been purposefully protected from the human race.

It has to be this way for we do not wish for humankind to destroy what is left of our magnificent old home. Neil, in your Subconscious is vast knowledge; in particular, a unique way of seeing the past lives for people, this being a high radio-frequency level, far greater than most humans could imagine.

So, there is no dilly-dallying now my friend, be not the doubting Thomas that you were back in 1701, when, despite your incredible psychic gifts you continued to doubt yourself over and over and never moved forward with any great degree. Elspeth pushed and pushed you for she also had the knowledge.

Your deep spiritual understanding requires you to constantly satisfy your thirst for knowledge.

Your fond love of history and languages stems from the higher understanding you had from your years of existence in Atlantis. You will be a guiding light to many and now we hope that you take these words to heart and act upon them in good faith."

Again my voice changed, it was softer, more gentle, as if this beautiful Archangel knew how to reach deep into the hearts of each of us.

"Welcome to the group Victoria, our little white witch as we lovingly call you. During this lifetime I speak of you were the delightfully happy one called Rosemary.

You had long blonde, almost white hair, with masses of beautiful ringlets. Your mother in that lifetime called you Rosemary because it meant 'wished for' child and most certainly you were friends to one and all, including the animals of the woods.

Spending many hours alone in the woods, you connected with fairies, spirit animals and other mystical creatures.

They trusted you and you trusted them to a point where you could communicate with them through thought. They gave you a vast knowledge of the mushrooms, wild berries and bark that grew in the woods. You also learned how to mix these wondrous plants to heal others with magical spells. They were spells used to heal and help but never to hinder. You were told by the creatures of the woods that if you used this knowledge for ill, your gifts would be taken from you.

On your 18th birthday you began working in a commune, run by an elderly woman called Elspeth; it was a place known for receiving healing, wisdom and love, and people would often come and stay a few days at a time. This is when you met Amanda, Helena, Neil and of course Elspeth.

Your delightful energy, your vibrancy, was gratefully received as you spread the joy of life itself. By sharing your gifts amongst the poor and needy, you brought great happiness to Elderberry Farm.

No harm ever came to the Farm while you were there, for along with your magical friends from the woods, you cast a spell that would protect all that were within the boundaries of the farm.

One night you had been out collecting berries and on your way home you noticed there was a full moon. You smiled because a full moon always made you sing with happiness.

You had stopped by a stile to look at the moon when all of a sudden a luminous vision appeared in front of your eyes, you blinked again and still the vision remained.

It was the figure of an ancient wizard. He smiled gently and by way of thought transference explained he was the Spirit of Knowledge for the Planets, Stars and Universe. He told you not to be afraid and that he was going to appear regularly and teach you all that was, all that is and all that was ever going to be. You believed him as you had always done with your forest friends. So began your tutoring on the much beloved subject of Astrology.

You could not have possibly known then that I was preparing you for a lifetime of work in this area and of course it is myself that was your teacher.

You started to use this knowledge as it was brought to you, to give people hope in often dismal times.

You had an affinity with children and could often be found amongst them picking flowers, laughing, singing and teaching them some of your ways; they loved you, everybody loved you.

At night, along with May, Thomas and Helen, you would sit in front of the fire and listen to Elspeth, who conveyed such unconditional love and wisdom that she truly did make your lives feel complete. Now my dear girl, we are not so far down the track when again you are together for the same reasons.

I'm sure you are aware that your role in this group of Chosen Ones is to bring your knowledge out into the open and use it to benefit humankind. You will be doing this with Elspeth. She will always be part of your spiritual life, as a mentor so to speak, and you can always lean on her for support.

Your path is defined and clear. You will continue to receive signals and messages from me, dearest Victoria.

I will give you the strength and belief that the path you are on is the one you so richly deserve."

On that note I felt my energy shift again, it really did feel strange, as I intuitively knew that Archangel Raziel would direct his next words into giving Amanda her message. Amanda is one of those outgoing, amazingly exotic women, taller than average, always dressing in bright colours and fabulous beads; a beautiful Soul inside and out. The following story of her life in Wisconsin is so contrary to the woman she is today, it is proof of our ability to grow with courage throughout the lifetimes we experience.

"Greetings to you, my sweet Amanda, so soft, gentle and quiet, tucked away reading, thinking, planning on how you could help the people on the commune. Your parents and brothers were taken as slaves and sent to Trinidad and on the day they were taken you were with them, but fortune favoured you, because your father pushed you down a hill as you and your family were being shepherded along. Although the slave marketeers had seen you fall, there were so many of you they could not be bothered to go after you. Your name was Helen, and you were a beautiful 16-year-old girl and if it had been daytime and not under the darkness of night, when faces could not be distinguished, you may have not been so fortunate. You were devastated, shocked, heartbroken, crying and running, falling over, no shoes, bloodied knees, you just kept running, right into the arms of none other than Elspeth, who was, at that very moment, on her evening walk with Thomas.

You looked in fear at Thomas but Elspeth opened her arms and embraced you, clucking away like your favourite mother hen who you had been attending to that morning.

With Thomas to help, you cut through the woods and back to the safety of the Farm where you would spend the next 47 years of your life. For quite some time, you stayed hidden in the farm house and Rosemary would try so hard to tempt you to go out into the sunshine and happiness. You never really recovered from losing your family, but with love and patience, Elspeth, along with the others, gave you hope. You were very gifted, my dear, and had enormous compassion and empathy for others as you do now to this very day.

It has been a huge task to bring all five of you back together and it is imperative that you continue on your path with meditation classes, as these skills will be called upon when you meet with the other four and begin the exciting years of working together once more. Do not worry about how this will all occur because just as this has happened, so also will the rest of the plan.

You are considered a very important cog in the wheel, my dear girl, so stay with us and you will be rewarded."

As Archangel Raziel finished speaking to Amanda, the whole of my body became so hot, I thought I would explode; as he had not spoken about my part in this lifetime, I knew the next words would be directed to me. He began by opening up to a path of knowledge I had not known before.

"Elspeth, your name means 'pledged to God' or as you know this powerful force to be, the Divine Spirit. My dear, old friend we have had so many lifetimes together, each one bringing you to the final journey home. It is with great joy that we on this side of the veil have finally got your attention.

You have some small challenges coming up for you, but you will overcome them and move on.

For now the time has arrived for you to finish the role you created for yourself all those thousands of years ago, your gift to humankind. Do not be ashamed or embarrassed to speak or write these words, for they are the simple truth. We know you have carried love and compassion with you throughout all your most important lifetimes. You have also had simple ordinary ones, but they have been equally as important for your Soul's growth.

Oh, how our hearts have ached for the things you have had to suffer, yet they have all been part of your blueprint plans, the challenges you put down for yourself, albeit at times with your free will interfering to cause you to stray from your path."

I opened my eyes to peek down at my recorder, hoping the batteries had not gone flat. Archangel Raziel continued on, the words flowing unrestrained through my voice box.

"Although people in your life today know you as Elizabeth, I shall always call you Elspeth, as you deserve to be called this old and beautiful name. You will have gathered by now that you have played a very important role in the lives of these Chosen Ones.

Yes, my friend, along with the support of your spiritual friends on this side of the veil, you have been able to gather your little flock to you again.

Listen to your higher self, Elspeth, for you have so much wisdom, kindness and selfless love; yet you give so little to yourself.

You have given over and over, lifetime after lifetime, lifting people to levels they would never have risen to if it had not been for your generous and beautiful love.

In many ways, this knowledge has not been without it is challenges.

You have had to overcome enormous hurdles to maintain your strong beliefs and convictions, which has led you from time to time to make decisions against your inner knowing. So, my dear, along with the support of your own Guides, myself and your friend Isis, we will begin. You have many things to teach and although we know it is not what you want to do, it is also not what you think it is.

You will be the Channel for us on this side to your friends and to the people we will be sending to you, or drawing you to, for healing and communications to us on this side.

Be not afraid my dear Elspeth, you will be guided.

Have faith and know that the answers will be provided for you.

In the lifetimes when you have held the position of a High Priestess or beloved leader, you have always shown a humility that we see as a great attribute."

As Archangel Raziel spoke, it was extremely hard for me to believe this was all happening, nevertheless I chose to keep the words flowing, there would be time enough later to dissect the reality from fantasy.

"In the life as Elspeth, you were known as a Druid Witch; but as you know, good witches were wise ones and so often persecuted by the ignorant. The love and compassion you showed towards Helena, Neil, Victoria and Amanda has never been forgotten by them and that is why each one of them felt so drawn towards you when you first met. You must not linger on the ones who have hurt you and broken your trust, for it is all a learning for them as well as yourself. Finally, my dear friend, we come to the specific role for you. You will continue to make yourself available to mentor your pupils of excellence. For even now they need the comforting and loving ways you have always afforded to them. That is who you are and always will be. There will come a time in the next few years when you have built the confidence in yourself and your little spiritual family, when you will begin to speak, explaining healing and teaching to the greater world."

I continued to allow this energy to flow through and out via my voice.

"Isis is here with me and would like you to remember the hand mirror she gave to you. The gift was to be a constant reminder of all that you are, and all that you will be. She reminds you to take tender care of yourself as you still have much to do.

We bid you farewell in this communication. We bid farewell to Helena, Victoria, Neil, Amanda and shower our blessings, love and light upon you all."

When I came to the end of this channel, I can only say I had an overwhelming feeling of reverence for the experience I had just encountered. Five years on as I write this amazing tale, every word has come true for each of us; we are yet to travel together, but I am in no doubt that it will happen.

When the Universe is ready.

Victoria is an Astrologer, and an accredited Level 2 Advanced Past Life Regression Hypnotherapist. Neil is a Healing Touch Practitioner and a certified Past Life Regression Facilitator. Amanda is also a successful certified Past Life Regression Facilitator and Meditation Practitioner. As for Helena, she is a Medical Intuitive healing Certified Clairvoyant Energy Healer, Crystal practitioner, and an accredited Level 2 Advanced Past Life Regression Hypnotherapist.

I do not know if anything more could have prepared me for the years ahead other than this extraordinary experience with Archangel Raziel.

Self-improvement can come at you in many different ways.

There certainly does not seem to be any one way in which to achieve this. Sometimes we do things for the wrong reasons, sometimes we do the wrong thing without even knowing we are doing something wrong.

We change when we realise that we want to believe in goodness, and to become a better human being, and to forgive ourselves no matter what. That is one of the reasons we are here, to learn forgiveness, non-judgement and unconditional love of self and others.

Remember that life is one step at a time, that we will have times when our intentions are good while at other times they are not so great. The challenge with intentions is that we cannot achieve good intentions from the outside, they have to come from within ourselves.

We will never be perfect, not one of us, not while we are learning. The real test is to accept our flaws and undertake to love ourselves anyway.

The challenge is to stick with it, to fight through the thick and thin of whatever is thrown at us on this Earth—the toughest boot camp in the universe.

Part 2

Tread Lightly, For You Will Travel Many Paths

"No one wants to die. Even people who want to go to heaven do not want to die to get there. And yet death is the destination we all share. No one has ever escaped it. And that is as it should be, because Death is very likely the single best invention of Life. It is Life's change agent. It clears out the old to make way for the new."

STEVE JOBS

Chapter 8
The All-Powerful Subconscious Mind

"The things that come to us easily, our propensities, are carried on a deep subconscious level into our next life. There are no coincidences."
Raquel Cepeda

Deep within each of us, there sits an expansive knowledge, not with our conscious awareness, but subconsciously. It is more powerful than you could possibly imagine. A simple way of explaining this is to see the Subconscious as a filing cabinet holding information on previous lifetimes, with a comprehensive knowing of the purpose for the current life we have. It also holds the memory of experiences we've had, past and present, and also extending into the future. It holds the understanding of all our relationships with family and friends, as well as the knowledge of all health issues.

It knows our true self and is always willing to be a supportive participant in our lives. The Subconscious is responsible for triggering intuition, and it helps guide us in fight-or-flight moments.

It assists us to be aware of values and priorities, and not to feel isolated and alone.

It could be seen as our most loyal companion throughout our life.

There are many things we take for granted, things that the Subconscious accomplishes minute by minute, including the functioning of the body itself and the all-important role it has in advising the conscious awareness on matters of importance.

Gut instinct!

The conscious mind goes about its day, using logic to perform functions; for example, making choices such as what to cook, cleaning, studying, travelling and so on. The Subconscious likes peace and quiet to communicate with us, so the art of meditation is a very soothing process to achieve a relaxation of the body and mind, and that is when its awareness filters through.

Communications with the Subconscious mind are always enlightening and throughout this book you will discover just how powerful they truly are. To communicate with this all-powerful, loving, non-judgemental, wondrous part of the mind is a miracle in itself, and it is entirely possible through direct communication that many problems can be resolved and overcome.

The Subconscious mind is very protective of you. It only wants the best and will do everything in its power to do just that.

However, there is a role we must play in all of this. We with our conscious/ego minds have to be ready to step up to the plate and be responsible for our own actions and thoughts.

This is usually when the ego steps in. It just loves to be in control and will be equally as strong in urging you to use your free will in making decisions based on whatever you want to feel. For example, if someone has hurt you emotionally, then usually you'll have chatter going on in your head, and eventually you will come up with a valid reason for being totally *in the right.*

The pride of ego is always on the line. It believes what you want it to believe. If you want to be depressed, it will be depressed with you, even though the Subconscious is sending messages to help you overcome whatever is upsetting you.

The ego is a very tempting energy to follow.

Another good example is anger and shame, again the ego will believe whatever you feed it.

However, there are positives to this part of the self, the ego, because just as equally, it sits as a safeguard and will work well in protecting your welfare, supporting you to overcome emotional distress whenever it may occur.

Throughout this book, you will see for yourself how exceedingly powerful this incredible part of 'the self' is. The Subconscious sits there providing total support and is concerned about the progress of the human journey you are on.

It is about using your inner power to be yourself, and knowing that while here on planet Earth you are here to learn and not be consumed be material possessions.

It is all about balance.

Chapter 9
Nadia

"Some things are so real you can feel them to your core. It doesn't matter where you go, they go with you. Anywhere."
Jessica Shrivington

Earth to Earth, ashes to ashes, dust to dust; for the body yes, but for the Soul?

So many books have been written on the subject of where we go when our Soul moves on after death. However, nothing could have prepared me for the regression Nadia was to encounter. Her voice was one of awe and wonder, in that safe and relaxed hypnosis, it would be impossible to have consciously or emotionally created the experience. The process of understanding these extraordinary moments is magical, especially when you have encountered Divine Beings of Light.

This experience was to become life-altering for Nadia. It happened at the end of a past life Nadia had seen, as she told me she was moving through light.

I asked her what she could see and hear.

The following are her own words.

"Where are you travelling to?"

"I'm leaving the body with a feeling of weightlessness as I'm being drawn to a bright light."

"How does it feel?"

"It feels safe and happy. My Guides are there to greet me including one I have not seen or known of before—Jazmahene—she has huge turquoise green eyes in the shape of almonds slanting upwards and a big head."

I noted a shift in Nadia's awareness, her face became serene, her smile radiating as if she was seeing something very special.

"My Guides are asking me something without speaking, I know what they are saying though, they are asking me to walk up the white stairs through to the temple which is sparkling white."

I ask her where it leads to.

"I'm being led into a large round room with a shiny white floor, there are many colourful crystals on the ceiling with a golden light shining through them. I'm standing in the centre as these crystals transmit their energy through to my Soul."

"How does that feel?" I ask.

"It is cleansing all the pain, hurt, illness from my etheric body and cellular memory. I feel light, I feel free."

There is a small frown on her face and I ask if she is worried. She replies that she is not and continues speaking.

"I'm feeling and seeing everything I have experienced in my life as well as everything that my Soul group have felt from my actions in relation to me."

"Do they ask you any questions about this?"

"I'm asked if there is anything I could have done better and if so, how?"

"How do you answer them?"

"I'm saying yes, there is."

"Why did you say yes to what you reviewed?"

"I did not like everything I saw and felt, but do not worry, I still feel safe and loved unconditionally."

"That's good, I'm happy for you," I reply.

"I'm being asked if I want to reincarnate into another body and I'm saying not yet, that I want to go to the Akashic Records."

The Akashic Records are records containing minute details of every word, thought or action we have made and these records are stored in a non-physical plane of existence.

The information connects us to every lifetime we have had.

The Subconscious mind, or Higher Self as it is also known, has access to this information, and that is why it is all-knowing.

"Why do you want to go to the Hall of Records?"

"I want to read the records and learn. I'm there now and the books, they are etheric books, they are floating from their position on the wall to be in front of me, it is amazing, it happens the second I think of the record I wish to read. This is so incredible, I'm able to either read it by feeling it or I can actually experience what was happening in the book."

"What is your reason for doing this?"

"I wish to learn so much more before I go back to Earth."

The regression finishes and I bring Nadia back to the here and now. We talked about that visit to the Hall of Records. In the post-discussion Nadia came to a realisation.

"I have now become aware that all my lives are connected, that every lesson I learn takes me one step closer to going back to my real home."

Nadia had unearthed her life purpose, and seeing her records in black and white gave her the determination for living a happy and fulfilling life.

She had experienced unconditional love at it is most precious.

Chapter 10
Scarlett

"Keep smiling, because life is a beautiful thing and there's so much to smile about."
Marylin Monroe

The many lives we experience are full of magical opportunities; they can be deep, complex and ancient, but always revealing, and only through the vast and amazing visionary adventures of a regression can we see how our lives intertwine so intricately.

Understanding why we are who we are helps us to live a happy, fulfilled life.

This is the story of a young woman who has been through many hardships in her current lifetime. Each time she has had to start over and struggle through new beginnings.

However, all we need do is ask for help, as the answers are always there. The human race in general are masters of critical thinking. Each of us will go through difficult times, but when we can better navigate the path we are on, then we have the chance to remain positive by reminding ourselves that there really is a light at the end of the tunnel.

Everything we experience is emotion-based and the cause of nearly all illness in some shape, manner or form.

Scarlett arrived for her session and it would be a fair enough statement to say she was a little skeptical.

I learned that she was in remission from an aggressive form of cancer and was to be married in a few months. What she really wanted to know was, would the cancer come back? What she found out, however, was enough to give her all the courage she needed to keep going.

She went smoothly into her regression, by going into a safe and relaxed hypnosis.

Immediately she is standing on a metal platform, she has no covering on her feet nor does she wear any form of embellishment. She is simply wearing flowing white clothing, her hair is long and blonde. I asked what she could see and she replied that the surroundings were dark.

"Which direction would you go to where you live?" I asked.

"Up," she replied.

"How do you get there?"

"I bounce and float."

I asked her to describe to me what she is seeing and experiencing.

"I live in an egg-shaped dwelling that floats in the Universe, I'm female and my name is Shantara. Inside my dwelling is one space, the furniture is timber and beautifully carved. I'm a creator of beautiful things."

I asked who did the carving.

"I do, I also paint," she replied.

"What do you eat?"

"I eat everything that is green, vegetables and herbs mostly."

I ask Shantara if she has a mother.

"My Mother lives in the next dwelling, her name is Kiora, we are very close and I seem to be happy with my existence. We all live in our own-egg shaped dwelling."

I ask what the shell of the dwelling is made from, and she replies that it is of a substance not known on Earth.

I move Shantara to a time further down the track and ask her to experience a momentous event.

"I'm being crowned as a Princess God, my mother and best friends are with me to celebrate, it is now my role to keep the people safe."

"Is this part of the Universe you live in safe?"

"Yes, it is, but there are others who try to take over our peaceful existence, so my role is always to negotiate, and sometimes it is very difficult to do this."

"I see. Do you have males on your planet who can do this for you?"

"We do, but they live separately to the female population."

The replies are simple and I have the feeling I'm not meant to go too deeply into this life. However, I do move Shantara again to another important event.

It is the day of her marriage.

I ask who she is to marry.

"Tan-Tae," she replies.

I see tears roll softly down from the corners of Scarlett's eyes. I ask her what is upsetting her and she tells me she recognises that Tan-Tae is the Soul of the same man she is to marry in a few months in her current lifetime as Scarlett. Tan-Tae grows vegetables and is a builder, and they are very happy.

As is often the case, we have shared many lifetimes with the same Soul. It is always a concern of the therapist about how deep to dig with questions. I have found that the client seems to control the way they answer, one always has the feeling at some point to not ask further questions. I believe it is because the client has received what is important to their current Soul growth.

I took Shantara to the end of that lifetime.

"I'm not very old, I have been killed, someone has strangled me from behind, I do not know who it is."

"How is the body being disposed of?" I asked.

"I have been wrapped in white cotton and floated out into space," Shantara replied.

It is helpful to our current life to know what we have learned from past lives and what the purpose of that lifetime was, so I was intrigued by her answer. It was quite obvious she came from another dimension, yet there were many emotional parallels with our lives on planet Earth.

"When looking at this life, what do you think your major lesson was?"

"To learn to love."

The answer was short and to the point.

"What words of wisdom might you give the people of planet Earth?"

"To be kind."

I thanked this magnificent energy named Shantara, sending her onwards along the journey I knew she would continue, somehow believing she would always touch the hearts and Souls of many others. Time was on my side, so I decided to take Scarlett to another lifetime, just to see what the Subconscious was ready to show her.

"I'm standing on a stone road, it is early morning, I'm wearing a vibrant yellow kaftan."

"What do you see as you look around?"

"Oh, it is so beautiful, the marketplace, it is so beautiful, there are so many colours, spices, smells. I love it."

"Why are you there?"

"I'm going to my stall."

The tone of voice was one of softness yet excitement, as if she was doing something she loved.

Self-realisation can be a wonderful thing, a knowing sinks into the consciousness, bringing about a level of awareness that gives long-lasting happiness. The desire to follow a dream can be strong and genuine, and sometimes we succeed, sometimes we fail. This is why regression works so much in our favour for advancing us on our path and purpose. The opportunity for the higher self and spirit world to encourage us, to support us, is a miracle.

I was curious to know what else she was wearing. She explained that most of her fingers are covered with rings attached to chains that cover the backs of her hands. Her waist is circled with gold belts with little bells strung along them. She described her feet; they are bare, apart from elaborate toe rings and anklets. She also described multiple piercings in her nose and her ears, with her arms covered with many bracelets and armbands.

So real was this to Scarlett, that her descriptions took my breath away. I asked her if she was carrying anything. In her hand she is carrying paint brushes. As she was describing this to me I could see her hands moving as if she was holding them. She went on to explain the male face she was painting. I asked her if she knew the subject.

"No, I do not know him personally."

I suggested that we go to where she lives, and on the way I learned that her name is Vishnu and that she is in her mid-20s and lives in India.

"Are you there yet, Vishnu?"

Vishnu explained to me that she is standing in front of a golden palace, a place she knows is her home. I asked her who her father was, and she told me he was the King. I suggested to her that we go inside the palace to discover who might live there.

Scarlett started crying out as she recognised people in her home from her current life. There were family, friends and staff alike with whom she immediately connected.

They were busy chatting and laughing, lazing about on colourful cushions and mats on the floor, eating delicious curries.

Scarlett cried out again, saying that she did not want to leave.

"I love it here, this is my real home."

A part of me wanted her to stay as well, as it became obvious she was experiencing a lifetime that meant a great deal to her.

Subtly, I urged her to go to where her mother was, and we found her in the kitchen as apparently she loved cooking, even though there was staff to do this in the palace. As her mother turned around, Scarlett began sobbing.

"It is her, it is her, it is my mother."

I swallowed hard to keep myself from joining in with the emotions, as I realised she recognised her mother from this lifetime. This form of regression allows the therapist to move a person to important times; times that are significant to the whole of their life. The person can move to any time and place, so their story is not always a natural timeline. At times they can move to a different lifetime altogether, so the therapist must remain alert to these changes.

I asked Vishnu to tell me about a special day in her life, one that she could remember with great excitement. It was Vishnu's graduation day—she had studied Fine Arts. I believe it may have been the College of Fine Arts in Chennai, the oldest fine arts university in India. I did ask the Spirit world and they said that this was correct. The King, being very proud of her, had given Vishnu a party and as a graduation gift allowed her to travel the world, to discover all that she loved in the world of art. For many years, Vishnu travelled through many countries, searching far and wide to discover opportunities to embrace her creativity. Paris was where she was drawn to and in that time became an art teacher as well as an eager pupil.

It was a life of happiness and joy.

Old age came and surrounded by her then many children and grandchildren, Princess Vishnu closed her eyes one last time.

At this stage I felt I had lived this entire life with her, it was so beautifully described. People were sad, yet happy as this death occurred. They knew this beautiful Soul had lived her life exactly as it was meant to be lived.

Vishnu's purpose in that life was to realise that she did not have to get caught, stuck so to speak, in a life that was not of her making.

She achieved this by following her dreams.

Chapter 11
Does Atlantis Exist?

"I'm going to run away," she said.
"Where to?"
"Atlantis," she said.
"Where's that?"
"No one really knows where it is," she said. "But I'll find it and then I'll go and then they'll worry."
Sara Winman

One day, about a year later, I was contacted by Scarlett again, the same young woman who had been to see me previously.

Sadly, she was still going through treatment for her cancer. Scarlett wanted to experience another regression. I had been wanting to find answers about a particular subject for quite a number of years and for some reason I felt she may be the one I would ask permission from. I wanted to question the Subconscious on a subject close to my heart, the truth about the existence of Atlantis. Never in my wildest dreams could I have imagined where this question was to take both of us.

Scarlett arrived on the appointed day and after listening to her own needs, I sought permission to make my own enquires, and so began this remarkable regression.

Entering into the past lifetime chosen by the Subconscious, she was a young girl standing on a shiny white surface, she was bare-footed, had blonde hair and was wearing a white soft gown.

Scarlett seemed very calm and at peace with herself and as I asked her to look about and describe what she could see, it became apparent that there were no buildings to speak of. This girl was standing in a marketplace, there were people milling about, selling beautiful things, tapestries and paintings, while others were reading and singing. I asked her what she was doing there and she replied that she was waiting for her mother, so while we waited I asked her where she slept.

"On the side," she replied.

"What do you mean, on the side?" I queried.

"You know, in my own pod."

"Do you have houses?"

"What's houses?"

I drew her away from wondering too much about this question by asking if she could see the sky.

"What's sky?" she asked.

At this point I was beginning to wonder how to ask the right questions. I asked what sort of food she ate. Brown, came back the answer. I knew better by now than to extend that line of enquiry.

"What do you see when you look ahead of you?"

"Pods, lots and lots of pods," came back the reply.

I asked if she had a father and was told he was the leader of the people.

They all dressed in the same type of clothing which she described as long white robes. The people would come together at the same time every day to chant before going to their pods to sleep. Taking her to a few years later, this young woman was being crowned as a Princess—her name was Shune and the crown was a circle made of gold and although not high, it had 16 different-coloured sparkling stones inlaid into the circle. Shune has become important, like her father the King.

Her mother's name was Marine and not of royal blood.

This seemed an important piece of information to tell me.

One day their area was invaded by insect-like creatures, they had come to hurt everyone.

I asked how she and her people protected themselves from these kinds of invasions, and was told they used the skin on their bodies.

"How can the skin protect you?"

"Because it is very tough."

"Does anybody get killed in this particular invasion?"

"Yes, the King."

Shune explained to me in a very matter-of-fact voice that although she was sad her father had been killed, it is something that happens; almost as if it was not an event so traumatic that she would suffer too much.

I asked what they did with the body of the King, and I was told he was taken to a special room.

"What happens to the body once it is in the room?" I asked.

"It just goes," she replied.

I decided to take her to the final day in this lifetime, and enquire as to what was happening.

"I'm being taken to the room."

"What are they carrying you on?"

"I'm not being carried, there are hands underneath me but not touching me. I'm floating."

"Are you aware you have died, are you frightened?"

"No, it is what it is."

"Now that you have died and you can look down from where you are, what can you see?"

"Water."

"That is so intriguing," I replied.

"Why did you have that lifetime, Princess Shune?"

"Allow me to correct you, I died a Queen."

"I do apologise Queen Shune, what was your purpose as Queen?"

"To reign supreme. I learned to be fair and just, like my father the King."

"Did you live in a place called Atlantis, Queen Shune?"

"Oh what a beautiful name, it sounds familiar."

"I imagine you came from a very peaceful and beautiful place."

"It was not always so peaceful, but beautiful nonetheless."

"Did you study, you know, learn anything?"

"Yes, I studied the laws."

I was preparing to move on from this life she had lived and asked if she was ready to leave. I got a resounding 'no' to my question, so I asked her what she would like to speak about.

"People need to learn peace."

"I see, will there ever be peace in future worlds?"

"No, however I tried to teach my people and they are very good, they are very peaceful people and even though we have enemies, we know how to be strong."

"Why does the enemy not like you?"

"Everybody has enemies."

"Where do they come from?"

"We are a kingdom and there are many other kingdoms."

"Right."

"I mean you are bound to have enemies, and as I am a Queen, I have decisions to make that will not always be popular."

"Thank you."

"Are there schools of learning in your kingdom?"

"Of course, there is magic, there are crystals, the people learn how to live, they learn how to craft, to make potions, many things."

I tell her I think that this information is amazing.

"I had children, a number of children, little girls, little boys, they were taught in the way of ruling and reigning."

"Oh, that sounds very important and a huge responsibility. What else would you like you tell me?"

"My throne is very beautiful, you can see though it, it is made of crystal."

"It must be full of energy."

"It grew, it grew from the bottom, it is clear and has no colour."

"How do you feel sitting on that throne, do you feel energy though your body?"

"Oh yes, I do."

"Do you hold something in your hand when you sit on the throne?"

"I carry something in my hand all the time."

"What do you carry?"

"A long golden staff with a crystal attached to the head."

"What is its purpose?"

"I can create anything I want."

"Can you give me an example of that?"

"I can give death, I can give life, I can create things."

"So you can make things appear?"

"I can make things appear, I can make things turn, I can do anything."

"Wow, that is extraordinary. I think you would use this very wisely?"

"It is not so extraordinary, but when I was young I was not so wise with using this power."

I laugh and go on to suggest that there are always lessons to learn using magic, when suddenly this beautiful Soul speaks again.

"It is not the same one, you know."

"Do you mean the same staff?"

"Yes, you are correct, it is not the same staff. My children each have one, they all have the same clear royal crystal. Only the Royal family can use this crystal."

"Who makes these staffs?"

"I do," she replied.

"I see, how do you make them appear?"

"They are just there, they grow, they come."

"Out of the ground?"

"There is no ground, but they grow."

I ask if she lives under the water and she tells me she does. I ask if she has scales, she does not.

"Can you see the water from where you live?"

"I can now, but not when I was younger."

You can imagine the difficulty I had forming my thoughts on how to question this extraordinary life, this extraordinary Soul. In hindsight, there may have been many questions that I could have asked, but in that moment, my mind was rather boggled from the answers I was receiving.

"But I'm intrigued a little as to how you are under the water, but you are not in the water."

"Because I can see the water," came back her frustrated reply.

"I hear what you're saying, but do you breathe in the water, or are you in a kind of pod in the water, so you have water around you?"

"I can do both, there is water and there is home, it is as far as the eye can see."

"Right, so they are all your kingdom?"

"No, there is my kingdom, and their kingdoms."

"How many people live in a kingdom?"

She replies that millions do, and again I ask if she is ready to leave. With a sigh say says she supposes, so I ask why she feels like she is not finished.

"I can go from where I am sitting on my throne and reach out and touch water if I wanted to."

"So you use your mind to create?"

"No, it is just how it is, there is water and there is not water."

"So in my world, this would be called magic, a magical craft that someone can use to do things. It is a miracle in my mind, because I come from a different dimension to you, somewhere very different. We all come from different places, places you do not even know exist, yet your home seems so magical to me, so amazing."

"It is just shiny white, nothing special."

I thank this beautiful creature, this amazing Soul on a journey that is way beyond my imagination and move on.

Sometime later, after I have asked the Subconscious questions on behalf of Scarlett, I have the opportunity to ask about Atlantis. This is how the story unfolded.

Before I ask questions for my own knowledge, I ask the Subconscious why Scarlett was shown that amazing life. The answer was absolute.

"To know that she is still as powerful."

Wow, I just want to keep delving into the life of this amazing young woman. But my quest to discover the existence of Atlantis is urging me on.

"Subconscious, where in the world is Atlantis, is it in England?"

"It is under the water, Atlantis is very large you know."

"Does it still exist?"

"Yes, of course, but you just can't go there, Atlantis is in bits and pieces."

"Does life still exist in Atlantis?"

"Of course, yes."

"Where is it then?"

"Many years ago, Atlantis was in Northern Iran, and it was soon to be all over the world and in many different parts of the world."

"Subconscious, do you talk to the Collective?"

"Doesn't everybody?"

"No, not everybody in their everyday life. Can you please ask them about Atlantis for me?"

"They do not pass out information willy-nilly you know. They do not tell everybody because they are not going to tell people things they are not ready to hear. It is not meant for you to know yet, but the time is coming, and then you can speak to me again."

"I was given information that a colleague of mine was Queen of Atlantis. Subconscious, is this right?"

"Well, yes, this is correct, but there were many kings and queens at different times in different parts of Atlantis in different parts of the world. It is not really a world as you would know one to be, it is their own world. For example, you could dig and dig below where you sit and find a part of Atlantis."

I falter for a moment trying to form a question that may lead me to a better understanding.

"Subconscious, if I was taken to that world, which I understand is highly unlikely, but if I was, could I see it with my human eyes?"

"Well, yes, you'd be taken by the appropriate people to a part that they think is right, similar to the one I showed Scarlett in the past life she just experienced."

"This is so hard to understand, Subconscious."

"It is ok, it is hard to explain to a human."

"Hopefully I will be taken there one day. We can leave this now and ask other questions if you like."

"You will be taken there, be patient."

I finished off this part of the questioning by saying that I have tried my best and extracting a promise to speak again on this very elusive subject. Think what you may from this, for myself it had been a remarkable opportunity to at least begin a journey of understanding.

Chapter 12
Isabella

"Those who overcome great challenges will be changed, and often in unexpected ways. For our struggles enter our lives as unwelcome guests, but they bring valuable gifts. And once the pain subsides, the gifts remain. These gifts are life's true treasures, bought at great price, but cannot be acquired in any other way."

Steve Goodier

What will she overcome for the greater learning of her spirit?

Isabella came into my life in the most unexpected of ways.

I had woken to a beautiful spring dawn, and decided to take an early morning walk in our local park to feed the baby ducks. On arrival, I could see the ducklings on the edge of the pond, and as I walked toward them, bread in hand, I could hear the sound of muffled crying. There was a woman sitting at one of the picnic tables, her head down and resting on her arms.

I caught her attention by calling out 'good morning', and as her head lifted I could plainly see a face betraying the saddest of expressions.

I asked if I could sit down for a moment and chat, and it was not long before I learned her name was Isabella.

After conversing for a while, she admitted that she'd found herself thinking of taking her own life.

Isabella was 45 years old, and in my humble opinion a very beautiful looking woman. I put my arm around her and asked gently what could possibly be so bad that she should think of taking such a radical step.

It seemed that in the past few days she had found herself thinking and remembering the difficulties she had created within her family circle. She went on to tell me she had learned how to downplay the guilt that hung over her these past few years, but no longer could the pretence be maintained, it was eating her up.

After some time I convinced her to hang on a bit longer, and I explained to her what I do as a Past Life Regression Hypnotherapist. I invited her to come and see me for a regression, without charge.

Somehow I knew answers would be found.

As you look upon the myriad of your own problems, I hope this story of Isabella will stand as a reminder that we are never lost or alone in our quest for overcoming remorse or judgement.

I discovered that Isabella's older sister, Marcy, was an extremely critical sister and the cause of all this trouble. She had always found a reason to tease and had a strong opinion on most things. What she didn't know was that her younger sister looked up to her and each time she teased and criticised Isabella, a part of Isabella's self worth was eroded away. This created a domino effect; Isabella began lying, stealing, cheating, always with the thought in mind that one day she could be as good as her sister. The trouble was that these habits became so normal, she did not know how to stop. Nor did her sister. The methods Marcy utilised to maintain her 'big sister entitlements' were only driving the stake deeper into Isabella's heart.

On the day of her appointment, I drove to collect Isabella. We went back to the park for the first part of the appointment, a perfect neutral environment. We spoke at length about her family and her place in the pecking order; there was a younger brother, mother, father and many aunts and uncles. In fact, it appeared on the surface to be a normal family. However, each time we touched on emotional issues it came back to her relationship with her sister. It was not close.

I explained that everyone comes from a less than perfect family, but that there is always something within us that longs to believe that we should be part of a family that is perfect and as life progresses the choices we make are naturally going to become apparent.

I also told her that everyone in her family, including herself, had a reason to be in that family, that they were all there to teach each other, and that none of them were 'worth' more than another. Jealously appeared to be an overriding issue. The hard part for Isabella was that she had now been intentionally excluded from her older sister's life.

She understood why and although it hurt a great deal, she knew she had done wrong and so felt she deserved the punishment. However, she also recognised she was a good person, and my role was to help her find forgiveness within herself. There is no doubt that as we get older and lead different lives, the closeness that is shared between siblings changes, sometimes even disappearing altogether.

Occasionally we discover it was never really there in the first place, and that it can be normal to not have deep family connections in later life.

So why were these two sisters in each other's lives now?

It was time to regress Isabella and discover the truth. Past life matters bring forward understandings of the purpose and lessons into each new lifetime until they are resolved. In the case of these two sisters, as I subsequently found out, the older one had been a vindictive sister in a previous life to such a degree she had made her younger sister's life an abject misery every step of the way.

The all-knowing Subconscious does not differentiate between each lifetime, it is such a powerful part of ourselves, one that holds all the knowledge and all the emotions, both positive and negative. Therefore, memories of the past can linger, causing inappropriate reactions to many issues.

Isabella arrived into her past life as a gentle, happy young girl. She lived in a beautifully decorated home where there were many servants to care for the family. Her father was a financier and very wealthy. She saw that she had an older sister, one that liked to use her power for her own gain. This older sister's greatest joy was teasing her younger sister, and would do so at every opportunity, making Isabella feel unworthy. It would be a huge lesson for this teasing sister. I guided Isabella to a time later on in that life to see how that teasing had affected her.

Isabella saw herself in a prison, pale and forlorn, and she saw that she had stolen a necklace, because she had wanted to look as beautiful as her older sister. She fell right into a trap set to make her look like the unfavourable one. I could see that this was upsetting Isabella so I took her to see her older self to uncover what destiny had brought about. She was living in another place now, somewhere in France I believe, and through the process of regression she found herself standing at the bedside of her sister. The atmosphere was cold and the relationship as unrelenting as it had been all those years earlier.

But Isabella could see that despite all of this her sister needed her, she was dying. Isabella was shocked to realise that it was her sister Marcy in this lifetime. She felt a strong and powerful, yet a confusing, connection to the scene, remembering it as if it were yesterday. She saw that her sister tolerated her because she had to, not because she loved her.

It was painful for Isabella to see, but it explained so much about how they felt about each other in this lifetime. Isabella realised she had never felt a loving connection but could now understand why.

Her purpose in that lifetime was to show her sister that no matter how much they may have been different, there was always time for forgiveness and acceptance.

Marcy's destiny in that life was to have a forgiving nature; the purpose, to love without judgement, to trust that God had a higher purpose and that she needed to learn of the pureness of love and understanding.

She died, not learning that lesson.

Isabella realised that her lesson in that lifetime was to stand up for herself. That she was enough as she was and did not need to steal, lie or cheat to be better.

She also did not learn her lessons.

As Isabella took her last breath at the end of that life, I encouraged her to move to the Spirit world.

She felt her Soul being pulled towards the Light and as she did she saw a beautiful glowing figure. I asked her who it was, and she replied, 'God'. He smiled at her and told her the life she had experienced was a lesson that she had chosen for herself, that she would again have the opportunity to repeat the lesson so that her Soul could move forward on its journey towards enlightenment.

It was for Isabella the most powerful experience she had ever had, to see God in his pure loving form.

I'm sure she will never forget that moment, as she learned that her evolving Soul would continue to exist through all of eternity.

Isabella understood that she and her sister would forever vibrate on the same level, and that it was destiny that had brought them back together this time, hopefully to set right their differences.

After the regression, Isabella spoke of understanding why she felt the way she did and in doing so I could see her resolve to change becoming stronger. Her instincts were sharpened and I was sure she would consider her actions more carefully from then on.

It may be that the distance remains between Isabella and Marcy, because she is not responsible for her older sister's lessons. This is something I feel we each might have to recognise at some point.

It is Isabella's reactions to current situations that are important, and her ability not to judge or allow her self-doubt to overshadow other aspects of her life.

It will have its challenges, she is still relatively young and has a lot of living still to do, they both have. I'm also sure there will be difficulties to deal with, and many more tears will come.

There will be times of heart-wrenching helplessness, but in all of that she now knows 'why' and that will be the difference between moving forward or staying in the same painful place.

I suspect there will be more lessons to come for both sisters, I also suspect God is looking on with great interest.

The greatest miracle of all is how Isabella realises now that no matter what, her sister will always be a part of her. She is finally comfortable with herself and her journey, with suicide far from her mind.

There is always a reason for everything, though at times you might feel like your very survival depends on a family member remaining in your life. The truth is we can live without each other, so long as we recognise our purpose for being here.

Past-life recall is a wonderful way to heal, especially when the Subconscious has its chance to speak as it did in this regression. Isabella's Subconscious provided some of the greatest wisdom I have heard to date.

It told her to take time and discover an inner self-understanding, so she could create a life of her own based on overcoming debilitating self-worth criticism and actions against her better judgement, which would then provide a sound testimony against the contrary view she had of herself.

None of us can know with certainty what someone else thinks of us, including family, and for many this can be a heavy burden.

You would not be human if you did not have some sense of self-doubt, and believe it or not, it can even have a positive effect when we realise this, because we become intuitively aware that we are all one. No longer will Isabella worry about what others think, in particular her obsessive concern over what her sister thinks.

It is my absolute belief that Isabella has graduated from her self-inflicted boot camp and is now more than ready to move forward to live a wonderful life, free from the burden of guilt.

Chapter 13
Magical Moments

"To live is the rarest thing in the world.
Most people exist, that is all."
Oscar Wilde

There are many ways in which to experience a past life, and not only through regression or hypnosis. With guidance, a person can see and experience someone else's past life simply by putting their hands on them. Hard to believe, but true. I had a student I will call Georgina, and this was to be her first experience reading in this manner.

Georgina stepped forward and placed her hands on her client's solar plexus and immediately felt a strong, cold wind and snow driving so hard, that she was forced to lean to one side and lift a hand to protect herself from the snow. The fact that she was only seeing this in her mind, was incredible to me and something I had not seen before, apart from an auto-suggestion with an 'on-stage hypnotherapist'.

But so real was the image she was sensing and experiencing, she was actually feeling the impact of the freezing cold wind and snow.

To do this without being hypnotised was something new to me.

Georgina saw the Spirit of a beautiful woman come forward to show she was protecting the person in that lifetime from a pack of wolves. Georgina was shown that that female Spirit and the animals were still the client's protection to this day.

Every life has a purpose and a reason for its existence, and as I mentioned earlier, there are several ways to see a past life.

Mediation is one, where we are guided by someone else to follow a path to a place and time. One can also channel someone's Guide and ask for a lifetime, which is a way I have used for many years.

The nature of the Soul's journey and our successes within this journey dictates how long we travel and to where the Soul will take us, lifetime after lifetime. Our Earthly relationships are momentary; however, each of us do have a family we travel with again and again. You may know of this as a Soul Family, a Kindred Spirit, or sometimes a Soul Mate, as we take on all forms of life, whether we be male, female or an animal.

Our connections never fade, as over these lifetimes we are there to teach each other lessons of patience, tolerance, self-worth, non-judgement and, most of all, unconditional love for self and others. Eventually, through trial and error, we do develop a strong understanding and deep love for each of our Soul Family members. The following story is fine example of this, one that is as astounding as it is magical.

This tale was revealed through the process of a regression and will be written without adjustment, for the reader to experience how two Souls, who have traversed through time and space, would be connected once more. The background to this story is interesting, and as you will see becomes part of the miracle.

I teach students from all over the world, and each one of them is special and unique. Jacinta is one of those students, and she came to my classes with a shy disposition.

It took some time to unravel her beautiful, bubbly self and when this was achieved, it was a glorious moment. One day, soon after Jacinta had been coming to class, I was speaking about unusual marks on the body, and how they could often be linked to a past life.

I asked the students to discuss any particular markings they might have on their own body, ones that seemed unusual or worrying. Jacinta spoke up, and showed us a small patch of eczema on her left elbow, one she had had since birth. Now, at age 29, Jacinta was frustrated that any amount of treatments had not cured the problem. I asked Jacinta if she would like me to regress her so that we could ask her Subconscious the cause of the patch of eczema, and to see if it could be cleared. We arranged an appointment for a few weeks' time.

The day arrived, and an excited Jacinta was ready to discover some answers. Without wasting a moment, we began the session. During the pre-interview, I asked Jacinta about her likes and loves in life. She spoke passionately about the ocean and told me she had always had a fascination with swordfish.

She could never have guessed how her story would pan out, and never in a zillion years would I have either.

Jacinta was about to experience an extremely vivid past life regression session. She became one of those amazing clients who come with a strong feeling that they have been somewhere before, or that they just 'had intuitive knowledge' about things, without knowing how. Often a client will write this off as simply having a passion for something, or that they have had a strange experience of déjà-vu or coincidental moment.

Jacinta was ready to participate in her past life regression, particularly to understand and remember the reason for her eczema, and fervently hoped to have her problem healed.

So, with that in mind, I set out to guide her to discover the answer.

I took Jacinta back and back in time until I was asking her to look around and tell me where she was. She was deep down in the ocean and she was a swordfish. I asked her what she was doing there and she told me that she was helping to care for the ocean. The images Jacinta saw had an incomparable sense of depth and clarity, it was as if the ocean had filled her awareness, having her believing that anything was possible at any moment. I knew with growing certainty that this life she was experiencing as a swordfish was important, and that we had made a valuable connection. I asked her to take me to where she was created, and to my surprise we went back to the 'Divine source'. She told me that is where all Souls are manifested and that when her time is over, she will go back to the Source to continue her Soul journey. At that moment, as Jacinta became aware that her spirit was immortal, tears rolled down her face.

I understood clearly that the Subconscious had brought forward this opportunity for Jacinta to understand her Soul journey and that the lifetime as a swordfish was likely to be an unrepeatable and enlightening experience. It was time to connect with the Subconscious. If this was real, it would blow Jacinta's mind, because not only did she speak of being a swordfish on a Soul journey, but for that be true, meant that somehow we as humankind have learned how Souls can travel in many forms.

As always, conversations with the Subconscious are as illuminating as they are informative. Jacinta's Subconscious was no exception, and with the conversation flowing smoothly, I asked it to remove the small patch of eczema Jacinta had spoken of. The response was a firm 'no', the Subconscious would not be removing it.

At the post-interview, Jacinta was shocked and surprised to learn she had been a swordfish, and I wasn't entirely convinced that she accepted this, but she was happy at the thought she may have been one. I had also asked the Subconscious how Jacinta could possibly believe this story and it told me it was leaving the patch of eczema as a reminder of her scales, and that in time, a bigger picture would unfold. The Subconscious had then moved quickly on past the subject.

A few weeks later, I received a call from a woman called Julie requesting an appointment. Her story really is a miracle. After the initial discussions, I guided her to the first past life. She saw herself as a fisherman. It was a balmy evening, the ocean was calm and extremely beautiful, and a full moon appeared to sitting on the line where the sky meets the water, casting brilliant beams that danced across the ocean.

The fisherman decided to go out on this night, not to fish, but to simply row his little wooden boat until he was able to sit right in the middle of the moonbeams.

Contemplating life and all that it was for him, he suddenly heard a splash and right before his eyes this magnificent swordfish leaped out of the water, its fin fully open, the reflection of the moonlight showing off the exquisite colours of a rainbow.

He was awe-struck and began crying; never in all his life had he seen anything so miraculous. The sight haunted him for the rest of his life, and on his death bed he was still speaking of this experience, such was his depth of love for that animal, one he had only seen for such a short moment.

I asked the Subconscious to tell Julie why it showed her this very special past life.

"You have always loved swordfish, Julie, and you've spoken to your daughter many times about this passion. The swordfish you saw in that lifetime as a fisherman is your daughter, Jacinta. If you ask her, she will show you her scales and tell you her story."

Can you imagine how I felt about this extraordinary statement?

Blissfully unaware of the role I was to play, this mother and daughter had come to see me independently, and in doing so, had unearthed a Soul connection between themselves that was almost beyond belief.

There were many tears that day. One can only imagine how often they would be speaking about this incredible miracle.

The connections are beyond extraordinary, and here we are thinking we are simply mere mortals.

These stories will perhaps begin to help you come to grips with the notion that we too have lived many magnificent lives.

Chapter 14
Curses and Consequences

"Those who pray for your downfall are concentrating negative thoughts towards you, without taking cognisance of the slippery ground in which they are standing, which could lead to their downfall."
– Michael Bassey Johnson

In the case of this story, I was still communicating with Scarlett's Subconscious, because I had another question to ask, and that was how best to send a Soul, locked into a curse against their will, to the Light. Over the years I have experimented using many methods to send lost and vagrant Souls to the Light, and in most cases, they have worked well. Although I have to say, that until the time of the following story I'd never experienced the consequences of curses and imprisoned Souls, but this was to be the doozy of all doozies. It took a while to unfold and before I set to telling you about the advice I received from the Subconscious on this matter, I'd like to share this unimaginable tale.

I had received an email from a young woman living in Pakistan. She wrote that her family were in crisis and asked if I could be of assistance, and she went on to explain in detail.

Dear Elizabeth,

My name is Azhaar, and I'm writing to see if you can help my family. My sister Bahja has been cursed through a black magic spell, and as a consequence of this shocking act, she has been bedridden for 11 years.

My family have tried everything, we have gone to the best exorcists in the land, even to the extent of flying across the country, thousands of miles from home. This was expensive and painstaking for us as Bahja was very weak, both physically and mentally, from the effects of this insidious curse. We are alone in this challenge as we live in a country that is not supportive of women, leaving very little opportunity to seek help.

The girl who did this to Bahja has been very clever and secretive about her endeavour. Through an innocent conversation, my sister Bahja has paid dearly for someone else's jealousy. I have learned through researching that there are many ways to do this, but in this instance, it was in the form of a simple cup of coffee. I believe a supernatural entity was invoked to create this mayhem.

As a family we do not know what to do, as Bahja's health has been worsening; she feels unbearable pain and cannot even stand the sunlight in her eyes, even showering has become an exhausting experience. Her dreams are horrific and constant.

You must know that I come from a place of pure love and what has happened to my sister Bahja is so foreign to our family. It began so innocently, it was during the summer period, close to exam time. Bahja was 14 years old back then and she had a best friend called Hessa.

They were classmates in school and most days they would walk hand in hand, usually with Hessa speaking about her trials and tribulations. Bahja would listen patiently while she complained about her parents and her bad relationship with them or talking about the boys she fancied and how she wanted to be friends with them and telling Bahja secrets that must never be repeated. After a while, Hessa felt regretful that Bahja knew so many things about her private life. There was a handsome boy in the neighbourhood that many girls fancied, however he only wanted to be friends with Bahja.

This made Hessa jealous, she didn't show her jealousy outwardly but she did everything she could to prevent them becoming friends, telling Bahja lots of lies about the boy and telling him lots of lies about Bahja.

Bahja completely believed these things so she avoided being in touch with that boy. But Hessa secretly became friends with him. During this time, I was busy studying for my university entrance exams and unfortunately didn't realise what was going on.

I didn't know anything about that boy and the negative role Hessa had in my sister's life, so was not able to see the volatile situation in play, and was not able to warn her that Hessa was not a true friend. One day, during this so-called friendship, Hessa invited my sister to her home on the pretext of studying together. She insisted that Bahja should drink a glass of coffee that she had prepared for afternoon tea. Later that evening Bahja told our parents that after drinking the coffee she'd felt something bad in her stomach but didn't know what it was.

From that point on, her stomach started to feel sore and burning and she started to suffer from constant feelings of nausea. As time went on, the situation got more complicated. She began to have difficulty leaving home, going to school, concentrating on studying, paying attention in the class and generally doing anything because she felt weak and tired most of the time. It was really strange and shocking to us because Bahja was usually a very happy girl full of energy for life. Now, 10 years on, she has changed so dramatically, to a deeply depressed, reclusive personality. My parents first took her to several physicians and psychologists. One appointment after another she was examined, taking many different tests; however, in the end, the doctors told us that she had no physical or psychological problems.

When Bahja began seeing dark faces coming at her in the night, she was very frightened, there were ugly creatures with torn clothes dancing in front of her, mocking and taunting. These occurrences seeded the thought with us that possibly black magic was at play. We began seeing a few religious men who are known to have special powers, even contacting witches and psychics and each time we were told that there was an entity with Bahja that was the cause of all these problems.

Sadly, none of them were able to remove this entity. However, one religious man did admit that the glass of coffee offered by Hessa was the main cause of this problem and that Hessa had used spells and curses on Bahja. A couple of years ago, Hessa left the country to live far away, even going to the extent of changing her name. One day recently, an email arrived from Hessa to Bahja, telling her that she was so happy she'd finally become successful in ruining her life, and was delighted to know she'd been able to make Bahja's life so miserable.

This is why I'm writing to you.

I sincerely hope you can help.

Yours sincerely,

Azhaar

So, it appeared that I was handed this problem to solve.

Having gone through every kind of method possible without success, I finally called on the big guns.

I asked my colleagues to help by doing a group healing.

So we chose a day and time; there were five healers involved from different parts of Australia and the world. Skype would be our connection. Olivia, one of my colleagues, was with me, which would prove to be fortuitous.

We began incantations using only powerful loving words, building up our light energy and sending it to Bahja's aura and to the room she was in. As we were doing this, Olivia watched as a black energy rose from Bahja's body, in a snake-like form. Up and up it went, slithering and hissing towards the ceiling.

Frightening as it was, we chose not to tell Bahja, but continued sending pure, loving light to that entity.

What was to happen next, will remain with me forever as a reminder that there is always a way to heal with the energy of love and light. Olivia was able to somehow connect with that black energy, and she watched it change into a young man. He was immediately humble and showed great relief as he apologised for being the cause of Bahja's illness.

He had been drawn against his will, through the spell cast by Hessa, to reside in Bahja's organs.

It had made him very sad and sorry.

I was grateful to Olivia that day. By some miracle, she was able to see this tortured energy, which is the reason why the healing was so successful. During this time, we had instructed Bahja to lie on her bed with her eyes closed, holding onto a crystal I had asked her sister Azhaar to purchase.

It was important for Bahja to remain calm.

To see her lying on her bed relaxed was amazing, considering the work we were doing.

Along with my colleagues, we sent a very grateful entity home to the Light in love and peace. As for Bahja? She felt happy enough to open the curtains in her bedroom and to begin making the jewellery she used to enjoy creating. I wrote to her recently and I'm happy to say she is living life as she was meant to, as a happy and lively young woman.

So, to close this chapter I shall tell you about the advice I received from the Subconscious about moving lost Souls on, be they cursed or not. I explained to the Subconscious that I had been asking the entities to 'go in the name of God and Jesus Christ to the Light in love and peace, where there is no judgement and only unconditional love' and that I would repeat this three times.

"You do not really need to do that," came the reply. "It is just love and kindness that is needed, one person might say get lost, go in love and light and off you go, everyone has their own tools, it's what you feel comfortable with."

"What about the mischievous ones, or the cursed ones?" I asked.

"They are annoying, aren't they? Well I just command that only love and light will be used until such time as they go. Letting them know I will not be frightened by them is what is best."

"I see."

"At the end of the day it is about love and kindness. Use love and kindness and you will always be able to help these Souls; they all want to go to the Light, sometimes they are afraid, or feel guilt, but they do not have to worry about this. There is only love in the Light."

I thanked the Subconscious and felt a great satisfaction as I know this is to the whole truth and nothing but the truth.

I had two more questions for the Subconscious, ones that I'm sure will be questions many of you have asked in your adult life. I wanted to know what happens to a Soul when they commit suicide and why are some babies stillborn, die at birth or a few days later?

Two days before the session with Scarlett, I had a client come to me for a past life regression, and his story led me to wanting answers to these questions.

The following chapter is Andy's story.

Chapter 15
THE CIRCLE OF LIFE

"That which is alive hath known death, and that which is dead can never die, for in the Circle of the Spirit life is naught and death is naught. Yea, all things live forever, though at times they sleep and are forgotten."
H. RIDER HAGGARD

ANDY ARRIVED AT HIS appointed time with an overriding question: he wanted to understand why he had issues with his mother.

I was pleased, in hindsight, that I hadn't initially dug deeper into this question, as I'd felt it would open up too many wounds before the session itself. I have always trusted the Subconscious to explain sensitive issues. The past life was met in darkness and I soon discovered why.

Andy saw himself as a female, lying in a four-poster wooden bed with dark drapes drawn to create total darkness. She lay there in a state of profound depression, having just lost a baby during the birth.

So forlorn was her state, it took a little while to encourage her away from the bed. I gently moved her to an important day, and it was the day of the baby's funeral and again the tears flowed.

It is crucial for me to be understanding and compassionate in these moments, because the client is experiencing the event on a very real level. Speaking softly, I expressed my condolences and it was not until I had asked if she had finished her grieving, and if she was ready to move on, did we leave the graveyard.

It was important to move to another day, though I did not expect to hear further sadness.

It was the day she committed suicide, such was her grief for the loss of her baby. I guided her past that moment and asked her what she may have learned from that experience and what the purpose was of having that lifetime. In both cases the answer came back as 'separation'. I guided her further, feeling intuitively that there was more for her to see, and as she arrived into the Light there was a 'being of light' waiting for her.

I asked her to ask its name.

"I'm Christian," the being of light replied.

I encouraged her to ask Christian who he was.

"I am the baby you lost."

Later, as I spoke to the Subconscious, I asked why it had showed Andy that lifetime. The reply came that it was for Andy to understand the loss his own mother had felt when she herself had lost a baby.

Andy's mother had never recovered from losing that child and after that she found it difficult to show love to her other children. On hearing this, Andy cried buckets of tears, as the realisation washed over him that he was able to finally understand his mother's grief.

Later when we spoke, he told me he had not spoken to his mother for 20 years and now felt he could let go of hurt and anger. He told me it was nearly her birthday so I asked if he would go and see her. Andy told me he wasn't ready to do that yet, but that he didn't harbour negative thoughts anymore.

I was so pleased for him.

After Andy left, I pondered on that life and saw how the circle of life is never ending.

Chapter 16
Questions for Alison's Subconscious

"Suicide is not a remedy."
– James A. Garfield

Some weeks after seeing Andy, a beautiful woman called Alison phoned to make an appointment. I had seen her years earlier, so I felt comfortable about asking permission from Alison to ask her Subconscious some important questions. Through this opportunity, I was able to learn more about the tough boot camp challenges presented to us on Earth. The past life Andy had experienced as the woman who suicided was uppermost on my mind, so I was keen to find out as much as possible about the outcomes of such an act.

"Subconscious, what happens to a person's Soul if they have committed suicide?"

"Like every other Soul who has taken their life, they are affected deeply by the action they took, it is unfortunate, but usually they require years of recovery."

"I see."

"If you like, they are kept in jars, they're not really, but just try and imagine this as an example. There is the nice Soul, the beautiful Soul, it grows in a beautiful shining light and when it is ready, it goes into another body. A sad or bad Soul goes into a jar, but it doesn't shine, it needs time to heal, time to repair, time to learn again. It gets sent back to another body after it heals, everything needs time to heal."

"When a person takes their life, do they have to come back and spend the amount of time they cheated themselves from experiencing; for example, say someone dies at 20 and they were meant to die at 25, do they have to come back and live that five years out?"

"Well, I do not think that is right."

I mention that there are so many mixed messages in our world and that this is a subject written about by many authors who have received channelled messages.

"That is their belief, it is what they want to believe, it is not necessarily what is true."

"Subconscious, I'm thinking about writing a book, and I do not wish to write anything that is going to cause fear, that's why I do ask about these things."

"Tell the people the Soul, be it good, bad or indifferent, needs time to repair, time to heal. It leaves when it is ready to leave, it could be the very next day that it launches into a new body, or there could be 1000 years of healing before it is ready, or it could heal overnight and spend time over in the Light learning. That is how it is, all Souls are part of the Light and they are all on journeys of discovery. It is not the big deal the people of today make it out to be."

"Thank you, Subconscious, I'm truly grateful for that answer. So while we are on the subject of Souls, if a baby is still born, dies at birth or a few days later, why is this so? What light can you cast onto this for the people?"

The reply came with surprising speed.

"That is a Soul who was not ready to come, one that was not healed enough. It is terribly unfortunate for those mothers and fathers."

"It is indeed, Subconscious, but why does the Soul come if it is not ready?"

"We all make mistakes you know, it is a very tricky world we live in. It is like a baby trying to walk before it is ready, or a singer trying to sing before they are trained; we try, we falter, we go back, we start again."

I thanked the Subconscious once again. It all sounded so right, so simple to understand. I knew from my experience in seeing and consoling so many parents that losing a baby was completely devastating.

I hoped this answer would help ease a parent's grief.

I wanted to continue with more questions, as I was eager to learn with an open mind. I didn't want to reject anything I heard out of hand, just because it didn't fit with my own opinions. I was prepared to accept knowledge from a wisdom far greater than my own.

"Do you think that today's operations, performed to insert foreign materials into the body; for example, metal, plastic, titanium, are safe and a natural thing to do?"

"Yes I do. Today we are fortunate that we live in a time when there are objects that can be put into the body to prolong and often save people's lives. It may not be right and it is not good, however, if you go back millions of years, people just died. So what is being done by medicine, it is prolonging people's lives and therefore building a lot more people.

We are becoming a larger society and a bigger world, so unfortunately all of this stuff is a necessity. Not everything can be healed with hands-on and distant healing. It certainly helps and it is a big part of it, but the effect of today's world, the smog, the food, the drink, well, just healing cannot fix all of that.

They need tablets, they need operations, they need injections, they are just things that the human needs now to combat today's environment. Dolores Cannon was right, it is toxic, it is horrible, but not everyone has that time, nor do they believe."

"Do you mean to say because people believe they can heal themselves?"

"Everyone believes it to a certain degree, but what's the point in teaching them if they do not want to learn?"

"But Subconscious, as you are aware, you are able to do a great amount of good work in healing the body?"

"The world today is just fraught with disease, accidents and trauma. Take people who have cancer, if they did not have treatment their lives would be shortened. They have to have the treatment, unfortunately it is toxic to the body. They would not have been able to survive without the medical work that was done by the physical doctors. Sometimes it takes the body longer to heal from the toxicity than it does from the event itself. Do you understand what I mean?"

"Yes, I do, Subconscious."

I thanked the Subconscious, satisfied that my question had been answered. Another subject close to my heart and one I speak often about in my role as a teacher is 'free will', so I was keen to have a fresh point of view. I proceeded to ask for an explanation on why free will is given to humans. It must be earned came the response. I asked how it was earned.

"It is what you learn before you come, you learn, you earn. It is like going school to study to become a doctor, before you enter this world, you learn, you earn. You come with free will."

"The free will to do whatever you want?"

"Well, no, not whatever you want, you have to learn, learn what is acceptable and what is not acceptable."

"So would this analogy be a good example? You have a choice to make, there are two paths, one will take you towards what you want, using your free will, the other will take you along a path that you instinctively know is right."

"It is not done without education, Elizabeth."

"Is the free will like a circle, one that you keep going around until you recognise that you are on the wrong path?"

"That is not free will!"

"What is it then?"

"That is utter confusion."

I can't help laughing out aloud, obviously I'm not being clear enough with my question.

"What's free will then, can you tell me?"

"Free will is being able to make a decision, be it right or wrong. You make your own choices, whether it's right, wrong or indifferent; that is free will. Free will is deciding to walk up a set of stairs, write a book. You lose free will if you are put in prison, but then again you used free will to get there in the first place. It is the same as what you're saying, but you make the decision before you actually get there. Do you understand?"

"Yes, I believe that is what I have been trying to say, that 'free will' takes you to an end result, through the decisions you make."

"Absolutely, that is correct. Yes, you *are* given this as a gift when you enter your world. You learn and you earn."

Because the Subconscious is so straight to the point, I want to make sure I ask my next question in the right way, so I say I'm a little hesitant in case I ask in the wrong way.

"For goodness sake, Elizabeth, what a silly thing to say."

"Then I have a question for you. Are there other planets similar to planet Earth?"

"Not really, this planet is something all on its own, but there are other planets."

"So are there those with oceans and mountains?"

"Yes, of course there are."

I say to the Subconscious that I believe ours to be the only planet with so much beauty.

"Oh, we have got everything here, but then you might go to another planet that has water and another planet that has trees, while another planet has nothing. They are all different."

"Thank you for that. I know we are seen as extraterrestrials by other energies, the same as we in fact regard them. Do these entities from other planets visit us here on Earth?"

"Yes, of course they do. We are the most populated planet in the Universe, so I do understand what you said before, but we are the only planet that has it all. We are very lucky. But we are also very hindered, as we have too many choices."

I agree with the Subconscious and continue with my questions.

"The temples, healing gardens, the Akashic Records, the near-death visual experiences people have, places that are seen in mediation, are these structures or places solid or are they similar to perhaps a hologram?"

"No, no, they are solid."

"Are they on other planets, or are they suspended in the atmosphere?"

"They can be, it's all perception."

"I see. For example, the Hall of Records, where is that situated?"

"Well, it is in Atlantis."

"So, in the Hall of Records, where all knowledge sits?"

"You know, I have to tell you, every world, every planet, has one of these, even the world we live in now. I say Atlantis, I do not know which Hall of Records you refer to, for example I could go back to Alison's many lifetimes she has led, and walk into many Halls of Records. Everyone has access to these places, Elizabeth."

"Can this be done through mediation? How can the average person access the Records?"

"In mediation, through regression, it is simply a matter of giving a person the right tools."

"So, as an example, I did regress someone recently, which led them to a Hall of Records. Once there they were able to think of something they wanted to read and it floated to sit in front of them to read. Was this right?"

"Perception, Elizabeth, it is their perception."

"So is it what you want to believe?"

"It is what you experience, it is what you see, it is what is realistic to you."

"I hear what you are saying to me and I'm sorry if my questions are silly."

"No, they are not silly. It is difficult to explain."

"Do you mean that nothing is real?"

"Not at all, what that lady experienced was very real for her, and there will be others that have exactly the same experience. We are a complex planet, a complex universe, we are complex creatures. You are only scratching the surface, Elizabeth."

I burst out laughing, because I know this to be so. I feel very much like a student speaking to a wise sage, and indeed I am.

"I wish I knew the right questions to ask you."

"It is not my surface you are scratching, you are scratching *at the* surface. You have a lot more to learn, but you are doing well for where you are. In every world, there is no one way, but in your field of work there is one tool and you are using it, you are doing it right. Everybody will have a different experience."

I ask if I can speak about the Planets.

"Yes, what do you want to know?"

"For example, my star sign is Cancer and Alison is Libran. Do the planets dictate our personalities, moods and so on? So many thousands of books have been written on this subject."

"It is all very true."

"Subconscious, we are coming to the end of our time together, is there something more you can share with me?"

"Nothing that I have not already given to you. Information will be given to you when it is needed, Elizabeth. In your field of work, information will be given to you until your purpose on this Earth has been completed. Look back to six years ago, you did not have the knowledge you have now, did you? You need to calm your mind, Elizabeth, relax, not everything is urgent, just calm yourself, and relax."

The Subconscious is right on this count. I feel such an urgency to give people a reason to live a vibrant, fulfilling life.

"Have faith, Elizabeth, you know you do not really need to speak with me, you already have it all within yourself. It is what it is and nothing will change within until you understand this about yourself."

The Subconscious has hit right on target, *again*.

"Take a chill pill, Elizabeth, do what makes you happy."

This amazing conversation has been so enlightening.

I feel grateful for the patience and wisdom offered to me and go on to say as much to Alison's Subconscious. I have regressed many people, and learned along the way that every Subconscious is capable of answering in the same vein.

Alison's Subconscious is right, we are a complex lot.

Advanced Past Life Regression Therapy, the method I developed, has proven time after time to be the catalyst to understanding that the information provided by the Subconscious is something the conscious mind would never have been able to give.

Chapter 17
A Heart-to-heart With a Celestial Sister

"Every beauty which is seen here by persons of perception resembles more than anything else that celestial source from which we all are come."
Michelangelo

Even before the Stone Age, man started to wonder about the heavens, the planets and weather. There were periods when sages and prophets, priests and kings alike, hailing from all corners of our beautiful world and throughout most cultures, were sought out to solve the mysterious heavens above. They began questioning the enigmas of the Universe, questions that are still unanswered to this very day. Einstein and Nostradamus were no different from the scientists of today, they have all been and still are adventurers, delving into the unknown, valiantly attempting to solve the truths and myths of the mystical Universe and all that it holds.

Never in a million years would I have believed I'd be speaking to a Celestial Sister from the Universe. You can be the judge of this truth. For me, there is no doubt in my mind. My only wish is that as I'm writing this amazing experience I can somehow describe to you the delicacy and musical softness of the voice of the one I will call Ualani.

This was meant to be a typical past life regression, but typical it was never going to be!

So allow me to draw you deep into this amazing journey, and travel with me far and wide to distant places, hopefully coming to a place of understanding in a way you may never have dreamed of.

"I'm in the Light, I have to go to the Light. I feel the heat, it is drawing me to the Light."

A very soft whisper, a voice in awe …

"It is pulsating, it is pulsating, the amber yellow is pulsating. It is like a heartbeat and I'm in this heartbeat and it is very warm. The heartbeat, it is very warm."

"What's happening now, who are they?"

"They are extraterrestrials, they look like tendrils, they look like the sparks you see when you look into a fire."

"What are they trying to convey to you?"

"They are pulsating again, I have to go with them."

"Do not worry, you will be safe."

"It is funny, they are forming into one, the tendrils are going into one because God is an extraterrestrial being."

"Did you say, God is an extraterrestrial being?"

"Yes."

"Am I speaking to God?"

"I'm not God."

"Who are you?"

"I am the tendril of God. The Scientologists were right, whoever runs them down is wrong."

"Do you mean to say the Scientologist religion is–"

"Yes, correct, but the humans who pass on this knowledge on today are not fully correct."

"Why don't you correct that knowledge now?"

"Because man fights the word God. Who said the word was God, who spelled it out?"

"I don't know," I replied.

"Man, man that is who."

"What is the correct word then?"

"Everywhere—Universe—Being—Divine Spirit."

She is weeping now and begins to chant the word 'Om'.

"Om is the word. [she chants the word again] Om is the tendril of God," she says in a very deep voice.

"The tendrils of Om reaches him, all of them reach him. Men put things in boxes, there is no Islam that is better than Christianity, there is nothing, everyone has equal right in the Universe. Everyone. It will take a long time for humans to learn that."

I tell her that it is difficult to understand, because there are so many schools of thought in our world, so I ask if love will overcome it all.

"Enlightenment will overcome that. Enlightenment will come from things discovered recently, mental enlightenment, spiritual enlightenment. But you have been chosen."

"Why have I been chosen?" I ask.

"Because the tendrils are always right, you have the tendrils that reach the Divine Spirit. Tendrils are not of man's makings or feelings. Greed, jealousy, is not meant to be, man has to work through that."

"What am I meant to be doing?" I ask after listening so intently to this incredible information.

"You are doing it. The tendrils are working through you, Elizabeth. You are bringing to life the beautiful pulsating light into the world, with the love and light of the Divine, with the love of [she begins to chant again, drawing the word out in a sound that is deep, full and reverberating] Om."

This sound vibrates as the energy drifts from her body. After moving Ualani to another place and time, I am again in awe of where we are.

"I am with the Celestial Princesses."

"That is so wonderful."

"They are greeting me, they are around me, they are changing, they are all female."

"What are they saying, are you one of them, are they welcoming you home, are they greeting you with joy?"

"They have a very high vibration when they speak."

"Can you understand them?"

"Yes."

"What are they saying?"

"They are singing, they are singing the heart chakra."

"How beautiful. What are you doing, lying down or standing up?"

"I am standing."

"Are they around you in a circle?"

"Yes."

"Can you feel their vibration going through you, as if you are healing?"

"Yes."

"Their voices must be so beautiful, all that love pouring into you, mending your heart chakra, is that how it feels?"

"Yes, it is just one single note."

In the next moment, the most beautiful angelic voice comes forth and begins speaking to me.

"We are the Celestial Princesses from the sky, when you see a beautiful cloud, it is us sending you a message, we make the cloud from underneath."

"How very beautiful that is. What other things do you do in the Universe?"

"I have to check if we can tell you."

"Ok."

"Father says we can tell you. We are the weather."

"Wow! Do you control the weather on planet Earth?"

"No, we do not control the weather."

"What do you have to do with the weather then, what do you mean you are the weather?"

"The weather is made from love."

"Oh, that is so beautiful."

"When there is no love, Father gets angry. We try and gather all the love and make beautiful clouds, not from here but in the Universe."

"Is that when we get bad storms, thunder and lightning?"

"Yes."

"Who is your Mother, who do refer to as Mother?"

"She has many forms, she comes as Quan Yin, you also know her as Mother Mary, she's my mother."

Ualani is crying softly now. "I want to go back," she says.

I can feel her emotions, it is so obvious, so exquisitely painful to see how affected she is by *being back home*.

"I know, but you have a job to do here on Earth, it is a very important task you have." Ualani is really weeping now.

"And Mother knows you can handle it, that's why she sent you."

Through her tears I hear, "She did not send me."

"Who sent you?" I ask.

"I volunteered to come," Ualani replies.

"That's very brave of you, but you know she supports you. She is always with you, keeping an eye on you."

Ualani continues to softly weep, and my heart is breaking for her very obvious awareness that she is from a very different and loving world. So I continue to comfort her as best as I can.

"It's very difficult to leave a place of love and come down to the tough Earth. It's very difficult, but you have support coming around you now, such as myself, Elizabeth, and people who understand so that your journey will not be so difficult."

Ualani continues to weep, I feel so sad for her.

"I understand, I really understand how painful that is, to not be with your Sisters in the Universe, in the atmosphere, where there is so much love and compassion and no hate or disorder. But you only put your hand up because you knew you could handle this and you've gone through those tough times and they have brought you to where you are now."

Ualani's weeps begin to settle and I ask if she understands what I'm saying and she agrees.

The angelic voice begins again.

"She knows that. Most people try to hurt, they do not realise the hurt, but the law of the Universe will always correct it."

I agree and then ask a question.

"Who am I speaking to? Quan Yin?"

"No."

"A Celestial Sister?"

Then there is silence for a few minutes.

"Best not to tell you now."

"That's ok, but can I ask what Ualani can do to protect herself here on Earth? Is there any advice you can give her to help her, to give her courage and support?"

"No, she is in a happy place, she will be all right."

"Do you have any more words to say?"

"No, we are looking after her."

"Well, thank you, I bow in respect and give my love to you."

Her voice has become stronger again and the words are beginning to flow.

"What has been said today must be kept quiet. When the time is right people will know they can change weather patterns through love; love is such a simple thing."

I agree with this beautiful being of light, it is true that love is a simple thing.

"People want things to be complicated, but they have to love themselves first and then each other and then it will seed everywhere. Whoever hurts another, the storm will come. Our Father is always fully aware. Man has funny names for things they cannot explain. But Zeus is not the Divine, Zeus is a tendril of the Divine, he is our Father. He says that those in a physical manifestation of evil, who try to hurt others, then pray to our Father and to us, and the weather will change. Elspeth?"

"Yes, I'm listening."

"I know you are worried when the winds come, just pray and we will hear you. Look out for rainbows."

It is my turn to weep now. I cannot stop the tears, because in the world of Spirit, I have always been known as Elspeth. Something I do not speak about openly.

"We all know you, that's all Father says I can say."

"Thank you."

"Elspeth?"

"Yes, I'm listening."

"Look outside the window, see the weather, Mother is crying."

Ualani is weeping once more and as I look outside the window it is raining.

"That's why she cries, when there is heavy rain and thunderstorms she knows Father is displeased."

"Yes, but she cannot handle the world, she can't control people's energies and emotions. But we can pray can't we?"

"Yes, yes, you have to, that is the secret, every human being needs to pray. They are so caught up with themselves."

"I will go out into the world to write and speak this truth."

"Yes, you have to. Look up into the sky, you will always see messages from the clouds."

"Bless you."

"You are blessed. Father says this is enough."

The Celestial Sisters sing as Ualani fades away from that experience, that beautiful memory, she is bringing back with her a knowing that she is looked after and protected.

Ualani is deep in regression here and when I ask her later what she remembers, her memory of the experience is blank. I tell her that when listening to the recording, she will be in for one big surprise.

I'm keen to speak to the Subconscious and ask why Ualani experienced this instead of going to a past life.

"Why did you show and tell Ualani about the tendrils of God, Quan Yin, the Celestial Sisters, what was there to learn from this experience?"

"She wanted to come down, she wanted to show people. She is Quan Yin's daughter. Quan Yin, she is Mother, she has 12 daughters. The funny thing is there are 12 Archangels."

"Is Ualani in human form called Ariel by her Celestial Sisters?"

"Why yes, how did you know?"

"I just felt it to be so."

"The Angels are the same as the princesses, it is difficult to explain. That is why the Christians say Angels are males with beautiful faces, but actually they are Celestial Princesses. Angels have men's names, because men named them."

I say that man can only do what man can do because it is very difficult for man to comprehend things.

Then comes a mighty laugh.

"What are you laughing at, is it what I'm saying to you?"

"No, I'm laughing at what the Divine is saying to me."

"Can you tell me what he is saying?"

"He said that the human world has a fixed fear that he has form, but he has no form."

"Oh. Subconscious, Ualani told me of an experience she had some 20 years ago while working in a hospital in France. A man came to the hospital and was put under observation. He needed to have a drip inserted and Ualani was asked to do this task. He was sleeping when she went into his room, but all of a sudden he sat bolt upright and said she was special and that she would learn something extraordinary about herself when the time was right. Does this story have something to do with this?"

"Yes, Ualani knows we sent someone earlier, he told her she would meet them all again. That was Father's idea."

"Was it, then that was a bit of humour, wasn't it?"

"Illness 'unknown' for that man, how funny was that?"

"I'd say that was the Universe doing its best work!"

"Yes, it was, she was told about this but she did not know what it was, but it was left in the Subconscious for me to keep."

"And now you have released the memory."

"I had to, they are all watching me. They are always checking on me."

"Ualani has been through difficult times, hasn't she?"

"I shall answer that with humour. Her sisters asked me to say that she asked for it."

"What do you mean?"

"She wanted to feel what it was like to be human and of course she has had a hard time. Some days they are killing themselves laughing, but their Father gets cross with them so they have to stop laughing."

"Goodness gracious, I guess it could be seen as funny, but it has not really been too much fun for her has it now?"

"Her Mother sends a message. The minute she cries, the Gods will come down. Her tears are the connection of rain. This is when Mother will come. When she cries we will come, but they have to be good tears, not handbag tears and all of that. Father says we won't come, otherwise we will throw lightning bolts."

"Oh dear, well try not to do that."

"No we won't, it is only a figure of speech."

"Is Ualani's health good?"

"She asked for it, she wanted to be human, so she has to feel the pain."

"Goodness, you're being a bit tough there aren't you?"

"No, her sisters are telling me to say that. I told them that when she gets back they will have a hard time. She will make them put their hands up to come down next time, with even worse hardships."

"Oh dear, that's a strong threat."

"Now her sisters are terrified that they will have to come down. The sisters say you *must* write that book, the title is so apt and they laugh so much when you say that title."

"Do you mean, *Earth—The Toughest Boot Camp In The Universe*?"

"Yes, they say they are not coming down, because it is too tough, but it is such a good book."

I laugh and say, "Let's see what happens down the track."

"So, Ualani wants to know what the purpose of her life is?"

"She is so funny, she put her hand up, this is her life purpose, she's got to go through the aches, pains and heartbreaks."

"Are you referring to anything in particular?"

"Yes, because she wanted to learn, her Father gave her a difficult lesson, she has to learn heartbreak. Heartbreak material with another human. Her Father does not tolerate humans hurting one another with bad intentions. He has unlocked this lesson for Ualani now, so no more heartbreak for her. Wouldn't it be funny if the human world was all female?"

I laugh and say there wouldn't be many children if this was the case.

"Yes, that is true. She has to teach, she doesn't know what she has to teach, but she knows so much and she does not want that, but it is all going to come out now. She is to teach people how to love, to help to change the weather."

"That's incredible information, Subconscious."

"Humans have to change themselves, and not sell their Souls. Look at the weather, if people sell their Souls, they need to keep topping up with drinks, drugs, gambling and so on. Elspeth, you were meant to come with the key and unlock all of this. Father is very happy so that is why you are meeting the family, meeting everybody. Ualani is going to get a shock."

"Why?"

She laughs out loud.

"Because she is terrified of lightning and thunder, she always runs and hides under the bed covers."

"Do you mean when she finds out who she is?"

"Yes, but let her know not to worry any more as Father will work it out for her. She had a dream, she was given a key, that key is you. She thought it was going to be a real key. There could be another key coming later."

"That sounds interesting, to say the least, I'm sure she will be intrigued by that information. Subconscious, Ualani has another question regarding the Soul. She wants to know how long the Soul takes before it goes back to the Source."

"There are Souls who are already back, but they chose to come down. Some Souls need to learn like a book, but each book is different."

"That is such a good analogy."

"Do you know, when you do bad things, pages are ripped out, that's when the book goes thin and you have to start again. You have to make sure your book is filled and not get your pages ripped out. Because if you haven't learned your lessons, all the pages go and you end up without a book. What's the point?"

"That is very good advice, thank you again for the amazing wisdom. Ualani also wants to know if Mother Earth can sustain herself with the population growing so fast?"

"No, she can't, because when the human people have love, then they will love the Earth. People have to be tolerant and not be greedy by having too many wives and children.

There should be equilibrium so they can do what is right for the Earth. There is a religion that says have more than one wife and many children and the men do not work. What's the point? If you look at two countries, one beside the other, one is green and luscious, the other, next door, is gravel with no trees, but lots of wives and children. What have they got? Hate, that's what they have, same land, different beliefs, do you see what I mean?"

"Subconscious, here in Australia, in the Outback, where there is so much drought, there is no war, or hate. The people are good people with big hearts, why is it that they have to suffer so much?"

"So much drought but not enough love, they plough the land, they take without giving love, if you take things without giving love, things can't grow. Love as in love, not fertiliser."

"Good god, there is so much to do," I reply.

"It is so easy."

And that was the end of this amazing session.

There is a lovely follow-up to this tale. I had flown to Darwin to see this client and on the way back to the airport, she said wouldn't it be funny if we saw a rainbow?

I looked out the window, and there right in front of my eyes was a rainbow. We laughed so hard, we nearly drove the car off the road.

A moment neither of us will ever forget.

Chapter 18

A Conversation With No Limits

"Faith consists in believing when it is beyond the power of reason to believe."
Voltaire

I am sitting in a chair by the side of a bed and my client, Matthew, is resting on the bed, ready to be regressed. A student of mine is sitting on the other side of the room, all set to hear a past life regression for the first time. Matthew is a left-brained and well-educated man.

He has just entered a past life and I can sense a palatable shift in emotions from him. I can feel my anticipation as the atmosphere in the room intensifies, signalling that something quite extraordinary is about to transpire. To maintain a sense of calm, I find myself telling Matthew to take some deep breaths and to not fear what lies ahead as I see his normally calm manner falter and he is finding it difficult to breathe.

"I cannot see anything. It's as if the area is white and nothing is here except it is cold."

Matthew is breathing faster now, almost as if he is transforming.

"I feel it in my bones, it is as if it is the very nature of this place. You cannot help but feel it."

I took a moment to think of how I could help him to move on from this.

"Take a few steps, you will find that not far from where you are standing is a more open and warm place," I said, leaning forward and whispering.

Observing him drawing breath and appearing more at ease, I ask him where he is.

"I'm in a forest, there are pine trees, the sky is beautiful, there is life all around me and I am whole," he says, with a sense of wonder and awe in his voice.

"What do you think you look like?"

"My body is light, very, very light."

"Are you in human form?"

"No, I am not human," he replies in a rather dignified voice.

"What are you doing in the forest then?"

"I look after it, ah yes, I'm an elemental."

I greet this with delight, I love speaking to elementals, they always have so much to share.

"What form does this work take?"

"I am the voice for all that lives in the forest, I have no name but you may call me Keeper, though I'm not the first keeper of this forest."

"I came from the place where all Souls come from. Sometimes we are given a choice and sometimes we are given duties. This time I have a duty."

"Were you happy about this role you were given?"

"Oh yes, extremely, but I was scared and terrified."

"Why?"

"I had no knowledge of what I was supposed to do. I was simply thrown into it."

"So how did you go about protecting the forest and all that lived within it, in other words how did you just arrive and start your work?"

"The forest told me what to do and then I began to help."

"I see. How do you help them?"

"If they need energy I provide it to them, but most of the time if they are looking for food or a place to sleep I guide them with light and energy."

"What do you love to do most of all?"

"I love all of nature, but there is one that I love looking after and that is the mighty oak tree."

"What is so special about this tree?"

"The oak tree was here before I came. It has been here since one or two before me. It is very, very old. Yes, this is where I get my information from. It is an ancient tree of knowledge, it does not talk, but gives images and feelings, from this understanding I then provide the healing and necessary energy."

"Do you have to rest your energy after helping and healing?"

"Yes, after a particularly hard time, or if I expend too much energy, then I must take refuge and rest."

"Do you know what a human is? Do they exist in your timeframe of life?"

"Yes, yes I know of humans. Time is different for us, we do not need timeframes to experience life the same way as humans do."

"Thank you for such wonderful insights."

"I'm grateful for the conversation, it gets lonely sometimes."

I'm still intrigued by the description this elemental mentioned when I first met him.

"When I met you earlier, you happened to be in a very cold place, where were you?"

"Yes, it was cold, chilly you might think, that is how it feels through the transition from the Source to Earth. In a manner of speaking, one must walk though it before coming here."

"Are you able to go back to the Source whenever you wish to?"

"No, we are not like other spirits. We are the elementals, therefore we are bound by the Father's request to the assignment given to us. We must fulfil our obligations and remain until our duty is completed."

"Do you have a lifespan, one that you die at the end of?"

The Keeper begins to laugh a deep-throated laugh and I apologise for such a human question.

"No, no, I'm not laughing at you. I'm laughing at the idea of it. We are not mortal, we are not omnipotent, no, no, no. I'll tell you a secret."

"Ok."

"I personally wander around in my form and do my work. Some prefer to take physical form, to feel, to understand part of what they are. We do not die in the same way as humans do, no, no, no, we simply disappear. Once we are finished our duty and the next one is ready to take our place, we simply go back."

"Keeper, when you go back to your world, is it far from this planet, or on the surface or underneath the planet?"

"It is a bit different in that it is neither. We do not go below it, nor do we go above it. We simply *vanish* and we go to where all Souls go, back to the Source."

"So you come from the Source and you go back to the Source?"

"Yes."

"Do you see humans as knowledgeable, Keeper?"

"Yes, yes, humans *are* knowledgeable, they know what they know, the only problem is that sometimes humans just make it complicated."

I agree with the Keeper and take him back to speaking about his role in caring for the forest. I want to know what types of animals lived there so I can have an idea of where the Keeper may have been.

"Ah yes, I look after deer, badgers, elks, sparrows, swallows and many others."

"Spiders too?" I ask.

"Yes, I look after spiders also," he replies.

"I wonder, Keeper, what is the spider's purpose?"

"Purpose of a spider? The spider is there to help. Like every other predator creature there must be a balance. As the lion is to the zebra, the spider must be to the other insects."

"Do they have an intelligence, the spider?"

"Yes, they do, oh yes, yes. Mother nature teaches me this, her children teach me and then in return I care for them."

"Do you speak with the spirit Mother Earth?"

"Oh, I do not talk to her like a human does, if that is what you mean. She simply sends feelings to me and when I feel this, I know I must do a duty."

"Does her spirit reside under the Earth?"

"She is the Earth. She is everything. There is no avoiding her, every living thing that breathes on this Earth is her child."

This response was so enlightened with an awareness; I was listening to the tenderness and respect the elemental felt for something way beyond our human comprehension.

"Oh, how beautiful, Keeper, I have a great respect for Mother Earth, and also for you."

"Then know that she respects you."

"Thank you."

I'm at the point where I do not wish to leave this conversation, the kindness and wisdom shared without expectation.

"Our time is coming to an end, dear Keeper, so would you like to provide me with some knowledge to share with the human race, something that is very important for them to understand?"

"The world is knowledgeable, they know, they know what is coming, so I will not add to that, but if I had to add one thing it would be this. Nature loves all and all should love nature. When you are taking from the forest you are taking from other creatures as well. When you cut down a tree, Mother is not angry that you cut down the tree, she is not upset at the human who has taken from the tree, she is upset at the lack of love you have for your brothers and sisters."

The Keeper pauses for a moment.

"I pass this on to the humans. Love nature because nature loves you."

This was said with the softest of whispers and I only just caught the words.

"Thank you, it has been such a privilege to speak with you. I realise that took a lot of energy from you."

"It was indeed a pleasure. Before I go know this, I watch all through the trees and no good deed for nature goes unnoticed and this goes towards you and the other."

The Keeper points to my colleague sitting in on this remarkable experience and then he begins to breathe deeply and I can see the energy of the beautiful elemental lifting out of Matthew's body.

His last word comes as if on the wisp of a slight breeze, like that of someone using their breath instead of their voice.

"Goodbye."

I sat back for a few moments looking across at my colleague, not able to find words that could adequately explain the past life we had just heard. Matthew has many questions for his Subconscious, two of them are particularly interesting and I know the answers will be of great delight to those of you who have psychic gifts.

"Did God walk the Earth?" I ask on Matthew's behalf.

The Subconscious does not hesitate to reply.

"Gods did not come from out of space and go 'poof'. They had to walk the Earth and see their own creation, to be sure the world was safe, not only Earth but other planets as well. There are many other life forms that came before humans, you know, but the Gods came when humans began to develop to see life from man's perspective and once that work was done, once they found that life could be sustained without themselves, they simply left. Although not all of them left, some remained and now you know them as legends."

"So you mean the gods that people pray to in countries such as India and China, Japan and other countries?"

"They are real, they are all there, you just call them by different names."

"Subconscious, another question that Matthew wants an answer to is why do some people have psychic gifts and not others?"

"This is a bit of a weird answer, are you ready for it?"

"Yes."

"This is God's way of compensating. Sometimes when you go through a really harsh past life or sometimes when you are going through current harsh times and you were not supposed to, that is their way of making up for that mistake and they make up for it by giving this extraordinary gift."

"Yes, I can see how that would make sense. Is Matthew's understanding of the levels of enlightenment correct?"

"Yes, you do not simply become enlightened overnight, it just does not pop in there so you can immediately think you are the most enlightened being in the world, it happens through levels. Everyone goes through it differently. There are many types of enlightenment, but the one that is the most well-known is that of course of the Spiritual enlightenment. The knowing, the understanding of all that goes on with life, you do not need to be hung up over it. There is life enlightenment, and there is athlete's enlightenment, to know their body so profoundly that they can understand every muscle in it. Then there is mental enlightenment; do you know of anyone who is alive today that has this?"

My colleague calls out 'Steven Hawking'.

"Yes, this is correct. It is not only knowing knowledge, it is being knowledge itself, it is as if you have understood all and therefore you must give back. This is mental enlightenment.

The Dali Lama, the Pope and all spiritual leaders, they are different in that their sense of spiritual enlightenment is different from most people. They want to connect with God, they want to connect with the Almighty being that is above every and all, that is their enlightenment."

The last question from Matthew is about HP Lovecraft, and from what I understand, he was a horror fiction author in his time.

"Was Lovecraft's views about the old ones correct?" I ask.

"Lovecraft was off the rails, his concept of reality was precarious to say the least, but he was not wrong about the old ones. There are many ancient and dark beings in the Universe, they are not to be trifled with. You will not see them in this lifetime." the Subconscious replied, with what I thought was a rather interesting answer.

I ask the Subconscious if they are the same energies that affect the unbalanced in our society, or the ones that come as nightmares as we sleep.

"No, these dark beings I speak of cannot hurt the human while we are watching."

I believe this to be so too.

More is unknown than known about these ancient and dark beings in the Universe, and in my humble opinion it should stay this way.

"The dark beings you speak of are cowards, they do not come from the old ones, they come from Souls on your Earth who have not gone to the Light. That is why they are cowards. But those of you who have been tempted to trifle with them have not had good experiences, and I advise strongly to leave this matter alone," the Subconscious continued firmly.

This answer reminds me of Hessa, the girl who cast the spell on Bahja. The faces Bahja saw were not the old ones, but a horrible mixture of fear and human intervention.

What our planet, this tough-learning boot camp needs most of all, is a solid grounding of faith, a knowing that love and the belief in all things positive conquers all.

Chapter 19

Past Lives *Are* Real—So is the Rainbow Serpent

"We are all visitors to this time, this place. We are just passing through. Our purpose here is to observe, to learn, to grow, to love... and then we return home."

Aboriginal proverb

For Indigenous Australians, the Rainbow Serpent is perhaps one of the most important Dreaming Stories. The serpent is known as the protector of the land, and of the people, and the source of all life. To some non-Indigenous Australians, this Creation Story is a myth, to be spun into an exciting tale around a camp fire.

The same could be said of reincarnations, or past lives as we know them to be. There are many people who do not believe in this, and it is mostly out of fear, although their beliefs around past lives are based on religious teachings.

This was definitely the case when Sophia came to see me for a past life regression. She had had a strict religious upbringing. Her husband had encouraged her to have this experience, yet the impetus for Sophia was not to see a past life, something she did not believe in, but to speak with her Subconscious and receive answers to all the questions that she carried inside of herself.

In fact, the first session was not successful because the ego part of her mind had decided it was well and truly going to control the situation.

These really are my all-time favourite types of clients, because not only do they challenge me to do my best, but it is the opportunity for a whole new world to open up for another human being.

Instead of pushing the issue, I spoke to Sophia about the ego part of herself, a part that was a vital and respectful part of who she was as a whole, yet a part that liked to control. We spoke about trust, fear of the unknown and a few simple ways to keep ego where it belonged, in order for the regression to work.

We arranged an appointment for the following day.

The next morning, Sophia arrived delightfully fresh and ready to embrace the experience ahead.

Soon after, she was in a beautiful state of relaxation, open to allowing the Subconscious to bring to the surface information that lay deep within.

Layer upon layer of information is stored in our memory, of past experiences, past lives, present life and even our lives into the future. We are highly evolved, complex beings of great magnitude and this need only be tapped into to see just how amazing we can be.

This is how Sophia's story unfolded as I guided her through the experience. With nothing more than a surprised exclamation, Sophia began describing how she looked and felt.

Her feet were small and chocolate brown in colour, and she told me she was a little Aboriginal girl. She saw herself frolicking in the sun with the other children. There was an old woman sitting by the river, it is her grandmother, and she is a healer. With a child-like voice, Sophia told me she is going to be like her grandmother one day. I asked her to tell me about what her grandmother has taught her. Her teachings were about The Dreaming, the Ancestor Spirits who came to the Earth in human form, and the creation of animals and plants. Sophia explained to me that she really loved to hear those stories.

Soon Sophia has introduced herself to me as Chikka and she is about 8 years old. She invited me to see where she sleeps, and I listened in awe as she described to me a small humpy made of animal skins, the floor inside layered with soft grass.

This is coming directly from a woman who does not believe in reincarnation.

Early evening has arrived and there is a fire in the camp. The Elders are relating Dreaming Stories, and Chikka tells me they are passing around important knowledge. They are singing and dancing and Chikka is very happy. We move forward a number of years later in Chikka's life, and she tells me it is her wedding day. She is with the women of her nation and they are painting her body in many different colours.

Sophia's face is beautiful as she smiles and tells me they are laughing and enjoying the opportunity to dress this lovely bride in a grass skirt. Then they have finished and she is walking to where the ceremony is to take place.

Tears begin to form at the corners of Sophia's eyes as she speaks of her husband. He is standing on one leg, the other one resting on his knee, holding a spear, and he is covered in paint while wearing many-coloured seed beads, and with feathers in his hair.

The wise man marries them and I ask what is going to happen next. Chikka tells me they are walking together, to consummate the marriage. This beautiful act takes place on animal skins by a warm fire, and then they are lying close together, feeling safe and protected. Sophia's voice was full of genuine love and I felt very privileged to have been the conduit in bringing such a beautiful memory to her awareness.

Afterwards, both Chikka and her new husband join their people for ceremonial dancing and celebrating. Then it is some years later in Chikka's life, and she is telling me she has her husband's head on her lap. He is dying, and she is sad but accepting, though worried at the same time because as she explains, she has many, many children. I learn there are six, which I imagine must feel many, when there are so many mouths to feed and no man to do the hunting now.

I say as much as I can to offer sympathy and support and gently ask what she is going to do with the body. Chikka asks me to wait while she goes off to get the wise man. Imagine that, Sophia is so into Chikka's life that she believes I'm really with her. I wait a moment in silence and soon after she arrives back with the old man.

They take her husband down to the river and lay his body on a platform covered in animal skins. There is a small green leaf fire burning at one end, and as the old man gently pushes the body out, she watches as the river takes him to spirit.

I bring Chikka forward to the last day of her life. She is very old and alone, everyone has gone, and when I ask where they have gone, she says they have all been killed.

I ask her who killed them. The answer came back: the white man. In fact, these white men are in Chikka's camp as we are speaking. I ask her what she is going to do, and she responds by saying she is going to the river. She walks slowly to the river.

"How do you look now?" I ask Chikka.

"My hair is long and white and I'm old and frail," she replies.

"Why are you walking into the river?"

"I'm walking into the river and I will just keep walking until I'm under the water. I do not come back out of the river. It is so beautiful, the eels and fish are smiling at me as I float along, I feel happy and peaceful, the weeds float slowly, and my hair is streaming back."

I encourage Chikka to experience her last breath and immediately she is rising rapidly into the sky. In the next moment, before I have any chance to speak further, a small cry comes from Sophia's mouth as she then relates to me that the rainbow serpent snake, in brilliant colours, is weaving around her.

As she tells me of its fluid and flowing movements, the joy on her face is priceless. I ask what is happening now, and Chikka sees a beautiful cloud shimmering in pink and gold enveloping her body. She feels she is being healed.

Sophia does not want to leave immediately, so I ask her what she believed was the purpose of that lifetime as Chikka. Sophia answers as if she were still Chikka and tells me it was to learn the nature of the land and the spirit of the land, that her purpose was to learn to accept and appreciate what Mother Earth could provide, to understand that no matter what she was given, she would always survive. You see, the greatest fear Sophia has in this lifetime is that her husband would die early and she would be left to care for her two daughters alone. Her husband today was her husband in that lifetime. I asked the Subconscious if there was a question it would have liked Sophia to ask.

The Subconscious replied that Sophia didn't ask about her old age.

"Your husband will live on to a very old age, and your later years will be full of joy and happiness. He is here with you in this lifetime to give you support, strength and love and he will never let you down."

This issue had held Sophia back from fully committing her 'self' to her husband.

After the session was over, Sophia was full of excitement and at the same time a wonderful energy had filled her, something she'd never felt before, as if she has been renewed.

I asked if she believed in past lives now, and I'm sure you can imagine her response.

I've since heard from Sophia. She is planning a trip to Uluru in Central Australia. It is a place sacred to the Pitjantjatjara nation who remind us it was forged by their ancestral beings during The Dreamings. When she told me she wanted to roll around in that red sandy dirt, to feel the strength and energy of the Spirit of Mother Earth she had me smiling in appreciation for her breakthrough in awareness, her new understanding of her true self.

I wonder if she will feel the spirit of her ancestors.

The message I garnered through listening to this Subconscious, is that there is a spirit inside all of us, one that yearns to just 'be' and when we can just 'be', then everything else falls into place, just like that.

This amazing story is a reminder that we have lived many and varied lives, leaving us in no doubt there is no room for the judgement of others in this world.

Chapter 20
Lucie

"Courage is the greatest of all virtues, because if you haven't courage, you may not have an opportunity to use any of the others."
Samuel Johnson

Lucie is 17 years old.

Anyone meeting her could not miss the way energy radiates from her aura.

One cannot help but feel safe and protected by her presence.

Lucie came to me with an armful of questions, some of which were going to lead her straight into powerful insights, to uncover the extraordinary person she was.

Revelations that would prove to me, once and for all, that death is very temporary and how our past lives are so connected to our present.

Building trust is an invaluable tool in this work, it is important to establish a connection to those parts beneath the hard-covered shell that most people build around themselves, to allow them the confidence to open up completely. Because of her youthful exuberance, and fearless attitude to life, it did not take long at all for Lucie to be in that place.

The most important outcome for anyone is to find answers to the 'I wonder?' questions.

Having completed the first stages of the regression, I was speaking to Lucie as she was seeing herself become part of a previous lifetime. Her voice changed suddenly, and became sharp and in control as if she was aware and highly alert.

"It's dark, I do not know where I am yet."

After establishing who she is, I know I'm speaking to Charlie, a Lieutenant who is the leader of an elite combat force. It's dark and Charlie is carrying a gun. He tells me he is at war, not in another country, but right there on the outskirts of New York City. He and his team are preparing to seek and destroy a gang of violent illegal weapons dealers.

There are 13 in the gang and eight in his team. I want to know more about the situation.

"We haven't seen them yet, they are dangerous men, importing and exporting weaponry, we work undercover for the United States government."

I say to Charlie that it sounds like dangerous work.

"It has its times," he replies.

"What happens after you find this gang, Charlie?"

"Three members of my team are killed and four of the dealers escape. The rest are shot, then we go back to base to complete our work before heading home."

Having finished the night's work, he asks if I would like to go with him to where he lives, and naturally I accept. It never ceases to amaze me that once a person is 'in' the lifetime they are experiencing, how very real it becomes to them. I know when the person I'm regressing is experiencing the realness of a past life, and this is important because I need to make sure that when a client listens back to their recorded session, that they have total confirmation the experience was authentic.

On the way to his home, Charlie explains to me that he has a wife called Kelly and two children, Toby and Sofia. It is not long before we arrive. It's a modern apartment and I'm interested to know about the style of the furniture and if there is a television. It's all very sleek and stylish, and there are a number of televisions. I ask if there are newspapers lying around.

I'm always excited if there is a newspaper because I can sometimes establish a date, allowing both my client and I to understand the timeframe of the lifetime they are experiencing.

"Can you see a newspaper, Charlie?"

"Yes, there are some lying on the coffee table."

"Can you read the name of the newspaper?"

"Yes, it's the *New York Times*," Charlie replied.

"Can you see a date on the newspaper?" I ask.

"It's hard to read, a bit blurry, no wait, I can, it says March 21, 1999."

I glance down at the client history sheet and attempt to do my maths while we are still talking. I'm about to realise something remarkable. That same night, Charlie finishes the evening meal with his family and as he is clearing the plates from the table, he collapses, having had a massive heart attack. He dies at just 25 years of age. Then I guide Charlie to look back on this life to see what it meant to him.

"I see that the dedication I had to my work in the special op team was everything to me, but what I should have learned is that family comes first," he says with an incredible amount of sadness.

"What else did you learn from that lifetime, Charlie?"

"I learned that anything is possible, no matter what your age."

A short time later I spoke to the Subconscious, keen to learn the reason for it bringing forward this particular lifetime.

"Subconscious, why show Lucie that lifetime, what does that have to do with her now?"

"It has always been her dream, she has always wanted to do something that was different. Lucie does not like all the girlie stuff, dresses, nails, make-up. She doesn't care about that stuff because it doesn't matter. What matters to Lucie is the protection of others. Her instinct to take control is the very reason I brought this life forward, as she does not like things going wrong. In this lifetime, she needs to remember to stand back and allow others to learn from their own mistakes."

I ask the Subconscious if that lifetime was the last Lucie had experienced.

"Yes, this is correct, she was only back here for a few human months."

"Subconscious, does that mean her wife and children are still alive in New York today?"

"Yes," replied the Subconscious, "this is correct."

"How do you think Lucie will cope with this information?"

"She is sensible, she will understand. Being in the army cadets is helping her to feel needed, by taking care of others. This will be her role in this lifetime too, but what she has to be mindful of is staying focused. She is very observant, she hears, see and smells things way before anyone else. She needs to slow her mind and clear her head to allow sound decisions to take place."

I moved Lucie to another lifetime where she was a protector of many people, those who had experienced racism, harassment, death, hatred and warfare.

After I had brought Lucie out of the regression, and we had the chance to discuss the past lives she'd seen. We concluded that her strong feelings of wanting to watch over her friends and family in this lifetime was a result of what she had experienced in previous lives.

Chapter 21
Left Brain, Right Brain

"When you view your world exclusively through the lens of Subconscious, your prescription will never be strong enough."
Jay Nichols

Regressing a left-brain thinker has its challenges. The left side of the brain is the verbal and analytical part of intelligence, so it likes to leave little or nothing to chance. It mostly requires scientific proof of any facts. Left-brain people are generally savvy, logical and methodical observers of thought. Scientists have now realised that children's and adult's brains can retain impressive powers of 'neuroplasticity', which in simple terms is the ability for the brain to adapt and change.

Having regressed left-brained thinkers such as engineers, doctors, architects and philosophers alike, I like to believe I have been rather successful in navigating the extremely complex path to the creative side of their data-processing intellect.

Carmel made sure I understood right up front that she was hard-wired to a scientific way of thinking. To give her credit, she told me she was a student of psychology, but had come with an open mind.

Her comment did give me cause to smile, because from past experience, I know that the Subconscious has a vastly different approach to the process of thought.

At first she was reluctant to believe she was experiencing anything and told me as much, saying it was her imagination at play. I encouraged her to trust the process and allow me to be the best judge of the situation. Before long, this young psychologist was walking through a marketplace, eyeing off coloured fabrics, picking up beautiful leather goods and telling me how she could smell the animals ahead. As we walked towards them, I could see her nose twitching in disgust at the smell of the animals obviously lingering in the air. I always smile when I see this kind of physical reaction because it is a sure sign someone is experiencing the moment. Now walking from the marketplace to where she lives, Carmel weaved quickly through narrow cobbled streets where she says the houses are built close together and are made of similar stone-like materials. We arrive at her home and after showing no particular interest in the outside, she walks inside and tells me the place lacks any sort of warm, loving atmosphere.

The walls in the house are clad in a darkish brown, smooth clay substance, the interior has a narrow stone staircase, a basic kitchen with copper jugs on a wooden table and a community courtyard shared by others.

We go upstairs to where she sleeps and there is a row of beds, none of which she can say is her very own.

Carmel is in this strange world now, so foreign to her current life, that guiding her to various parts of the house takes skill.

Recognising when to stop, look and examine is important, while at the same time I have to make sure my curiosity does not travel so far as to interrupt the experience she is having.

By following my instincts, she is now standing in a room that sounds to me like a classroom. There are small wooden desks and a single desk and chair at the front. On that desk is a leather-bound book with a gold inscription inlaid deep into the front cover and in a dialect that is difficult for her to decipher. From her own observations, it appears the symbols might be perhaps of ancient Hebrew or a similar language.

I attempt to establish her name and age without directly asking, but in the case of this regression, it is as if she is a ghost walking into the past, completely absorbed in that life.

Carmel tells me there is no-one in the house, and so I guide her forward to another time in her life. She is standing in front of an old stone church, and I encourage her to look inside the window. This she does and sees many people enjoying a celebration of sorts. Being the curious voyeur that I am, I urge her to walk into the church.

Low and behold the people are celebrating the crowning of a King. It is such a joyous occasion and she is in awe of the beauty, the joy, the absolute magnificence of the moment.

As she is watching this event and not part of the occasion, it seemed appropriate to move her to another time and place. It is a few years later and she is once again in the market. I encourage her to go to where she lives. She's immediately standing outside a baker's shop, where there are older women wearing long white aprons and scarfs on their heads pulling huge round loaves of bread out of wood-fired ovens.

"Would you like to go in and buy a loaf of that bread?" I ask.

"Yes, I'll do that," she replies, and she walks straight into the shop.

I can see that the aroma of freshly baked bread has her drawing in deep breaths, appreciating that delicious smell of yeast, something, I imagine, would be hanging heavily in the air.

"What does your money look like, what shape and colour is it?"

Her coins are round in shape and dirty in colour. At this point of the regression, Carmel is regressed so deeply that she has fully connected to this lifetime. Long gone is that questioning left-brained scholar, instead replaced by a higher part of herself that is all-knowing, ripened with layered memories of her past life experiences.

With the loaf of bread in hand, she leaves the shop and begins to walk up a set of stairs to her apartment, one that sits above the shop.

You will soon see where this story is heading. In its entirety you may not think it particularly interesting, but like all of our life experiences, there is a light of understanding at the end of every tunnel.

The apartment is compact and the bedroom she goes into has a similar row of beds to the last place she had lived in. This time, however, she is a carer for orphaned children.

I suggest to her that it sounds as if she has a lot of responsibility in caring for the children and I'm interested in how she has enough money to care for herself and the others.

Carmel is a dressmaker and travels to the old marketplace each day to sell her work and to offer to mend people's clothes.

On the last day of her life she is surrounded by many of the orphaned children she had cared for. Her death is peaceful and she is at an old age, she is not afraid of what lies ahead. With her last breath taken, I ask the Soul that has lifted from the body the all-important question.

"What was the purpose of your life, why did you choose such a difficult one to experience?"

"I needed to become more caring. By having a hard life, I gave myself many lessons to learn about the hardship of others."

I found her response to be extremely humble.

Later, when I was speaking to the rather shy Subconscious, I sought to have many questions answered for my client about this particular life, one that appeared to be so far removed from Carmel's lifetime today.

"What was so important about that church, Subconscious? It didn't appear relevant to the life she was seeing?"

"It was important for her to see the way society can be good. He was a loving King and the people were all happy together. Carmel was able to see how important happiness was and for her, it was one of the first times she was truly happy."

“What *was* her name, and was she an orphan herself?”

The Subconscious chuckled warmly and acknowledged she was expecting this question. I tell her that Carmel would be intrigued and the Subconscious agrees wholeheartedly.

“Well, yes you are right, she was orphaned. Her name was Hannah.”

“Are my assumptions correct, that the words on the front of that book were Hebrew and that Israel was her home?”

“Yes, you are right.”

Carmel had many questions for her Subconscious and as you will soon see, the past life she experienced was to have a powerful bearing on her life today.

I proceeded to ask Carmel’s questions.

“Subconscious, Carmel wants to know what it means to live a good life?”

“To live a good life is to feel fulfilled in your purpose for life itself. To feel good self-worth, to feel happy for those around you, to feel that you have done everything that you can do. It changes with different people.”

“What would you like Carmel to believe in?” I ask.

“In anything she needs to know. Carmel needs to understand people’s behaviours from a less scientific point of view, to learn of other reasons behind their different behaviours, not just the science behind it.”

“What can you tell Carmel to boost her self-worth?”

“She is a very beautiful Soul. She was put on this Earth to help people in this lifetime, as she has done in many previous lifetimes. She still has the role of a caregiver and people are drawn to her. She is a very light person.”

“Subconscious, can you tell Carmel about her family and why she chose her particular parents, because she worries so much about losing them before their time?”

"Carmel and her family are very happy and they should be, she does not need to feel fearful for she will meet them again. Her parents will always look over her. She chose her parents for a very special reason. Carmel was very used to looking after other people, and it was her turn to be looked after. They are very loving parents and were the best fit to look after her, to love her, to bring her up in the most loving environment possible."

"What a beautiful answer, Subconscious, I know Carmel will love to hear this. Do you think Carmel should continue to believe proven scientific fact is the answer for the work that she does?"

"I think because she has always believed in a scientific way of life, she should keep with it. It is what she has always grown up believing, and changing that now would cause havoc. This time with you has changed her a bit, the stories you will relate to her will give her a different way of looking at things."

"Do you have any last advice for Carmel, Subconscious, as this is probably the only opportunity you will ever have, so be open and tell her how you feel."

"I am very glad we have done this, she is quite closed sometimes and it is difficult for me to explain everything, as it is not what she wants to hear, I believe. I think sometimes she should be more selfish, not a lot, but to take more time to do things for herself. She should always continue to be kind. In this day and age, it is hard for society to remember kindness. Kindness can take people very far. She must study hard, but not get too sidetracked, too focused, and most of all allow herself to be loved."

"Thank you so much, Subconscious, you have been very kind and thoughtful. I asked for Carmel's permission to ask you a question for my own interest. Do I have your permission to ask a question?"

Generously, the Subconscious granted approval.

"Fear is a great challenge to many humans. I do not speak of the fight-or-flight fear, but those fears that hold us back from moving forward. Can you explain this type of fear and how we might overcome such anxious emotions?"

"Fear comes from the moment the Soul is born and is something that is very, very deeply innate in each of us. All humans have a fear that passes from one lifetime to the next and that fear can grow. When we learn to deal with the fear, it lessens in our following lives. Sometimes these fears can evolve into other fears, but, generally speaking, each person will have one or two fears that stay with them through each of their lifetimes."

Not fully comprehending why anyone would be crazy enough to bring any kind of fear forward with them into a new lifetime, I ask the Subconscious why people do this.

"It is the way in which people can grow; the fears are there to teach us lessons, for us to become more resilient, for us to learn how to fight against these fears."

"Do you think that fear leads to bad actions?"

"Yes."

"Subconscious, would you agree that the people of our world are caught up in racial tensions that are so threatening that it is leading them towards greater fears and anxieties? What do you think about all of this prejudice, man against man, so to speak?"

"I think it is deeply saddening, and many of the emotions revolve around fear, so today, people are fearful because of these racial tensions. Tensions that provoke anger, tensions that provoke sadness."

"Do you think the world can change to become a better place?"

"I believe the world will change to become a *different place,* maybe better in some people's eyes and for others it will not be so good. The world is constantly evolving."

"Yes, I agree with you, Subconscious. Are our fears evolving and growing, is that what you mean?"

"Changing. As our society changes, people's fears will change. For instance, once upon a time we were fearful of being hit by a car. Now we are fearful of how people will react. It is all very sad and much worse than it ever was."

"That brings me to another question about Truth. Do you think people lie because of their fears?"

"I believe people lie to protect themselves and those around them, usually because they are fearful of the consequences."

"Is lying such a bad thing?"

"Not always, people have told lies for good reasons."

As we came to the end of this amazing regression, I asked the Subconscious to describe itself.

Now remember I have been speaking to a young woman who is highly intelligent, a woman who bases her thoughts and theories on solid scientific facts.

"I am all present and I am all knowing."

I smiled when I heard this, for again it proves that we each carry all the knowledge we seek within our own self.

I asked the Subconscious how often Carmel should listen to the regression.

"She should continue to listen to it all through her life as a reminder that the focus is not always scientific, so that she keeps her mind broad, helping her to see things from all directions."

The upshot for Carmel, in listening back to that regression, was that it left her at a loss for words. Most people will remember most of their experience, but she did not remember any of the conversations nor the past life she had experienced.

It was quite a revelation to her.

I was personally pleased about this, because it was an indication that I had connected to her soft, gentle higher self, the part of Carmel that allowed her to access information and wisdom that otherwise would have been impossible to connect with through her rational mind.

As for Carmel, in taking that opportunity to assimilate her Subconscious mind, to listen to that intuitive intelligent part of herself, combined with all of her past learning, has allowed her to come to realise just how powerful she is and how she *will* be able to make a difference to her life journey and to others in the world at large.

These amazing stories I'm sharing with you are very real.

Journeys of enlightened understanding bring a rich and vibrant acknowledgement of who we truly are. This knowledge, this amazing wisdom that lies within, is deep-rooted and can never be destroyed, no matter what happens to us.

We can be judged, abused, made to feel worthless, hung, drawn and quartered as the saying goes, but there is nothing, nor anyone, that can destroy the magnificent Soul that is our true essence. What greater way is there to learn, than by learning through life experiences? I'm reminded of this by the hundreds of Subconscious minds I have spoken to who call themselves names such as, 'all knowing', 'light', 'gentle love', 'powerful wisdom', endless beautiful names. I have never heard a negative response.

Failures, disappointments, poverty, anger, judgements?

These are emotions and experiences created by ourselves to learn from. Sadly, there are those among us who use false powers in order to dictate, control and manipulate others.

How can I be sure of saying this?

I have had the greatest of opportunities by listening to all those astute, discriminating Subconscious minds. When I ask a Subconscious what was learnt by the person in whichever lifetime was revealed, without fail the answer always comes back in the same vein.

Regrets and realisations are among the many emotions the Soul experiences once it has passed from a lifetime. Then it can, from a place of non-judgement, reflect on its actions and how these actions affected those who were part of their lives. These actions also have an impact on the Soul's progress towards enlightenment.

Empathy, compassion, understanding and forgiveness pours from the hearts of people who have been hurt, murdered, maimed, betrayed and cheated by others, as they realise those experiences were there to help them grow. For the perpetrator, the lessons are ongoing, unless they learn and grow. It is a circle, and we have all experienced so many facets of learning.

The important thing to remember is that no matter what you have done or not done, do not make yourself sick over it. It is not worth it, because this is the reason you are here on this boot camp that is Earth.

You are loved, warts and all.

At the end of each lifetime, we do go home to the Light. There is no hell and damnation. For centuries these words have been used by those who want to keep us in a state of fearing the unknown. Finding our way through the tangled webs we have created takes patience, tenacity and resilience.

All these strengths lie within each of us.

How many times do you see people rise up from the ashes of adversity? They do not have super human powers any more than you do; they are simply people who have dug deep and found that part of themselves that is strong, the same part that lies within us all.

Just for one moment, close your eyes and imagine a handful of the tiniest of seeds. These seeds grow to produce flowers with unique fragrances; each one an umbilical cord that, incredibly, influences your perception of the Subconscious. With each breath you take of these beautiful fragrances, you create a unique experience not to be repeated by yourself or anyone else. These moments fill you with forgiveness, non-judgement, tranquility, integrity, prosperity, happiness, pride, peace and love. Children are a perfect examples of this, as they are so open to accepting the perfection and beauty that life has to offer.

Sadly, over time, children learn that not everything is pleasant, that less than desirable thing happen.

In doing so, they internalise these experiences until finally as adults they begin the vicious cycle of negativity all over again. We, as adults, certainly have an enormous responsibility.

As the seasons come and go, so too can you plant these seeds, over and over again, to create that perfection we all long for.

Self-judgement cannot hurt our Soul, it remains separate from our actions. For sure the Soul can be sad and require time to heal, but it is stoic in its nature, knowing that death is the opportunity to heal and move on.

Many of us put ourselves forward to learn harsh lessons, and recognising the sacrifice you have made to progress spiritually is the true essence of who you are.

Never lose focus on your journey, it is well within your ability to be a loving, happy Soul; in fact it is your magnificent right to transform, radiate, advance and be liberated here on Earth, the toughest boot camp in the universe.

Chapter 22
Meeting William Rogers

"There are no mistakes, no coincidences.
All events are blessings given to us to learn from."
– Elisabeth Kubler-Ross

Life is full of uncertainty.

It is how you handle the unexpected that is most important.

Life can be full of nervous apprehensions that stop you from living life to the fullest, or life can change in the blink of an eye and leave you wondering at the challenges with which you have been presented and asking yourself, 'Why has this happened to me?'

I believe this to be something that effects every single human at some point in their lives.

But if you can come to terms with this prospect, long before anything ever happens, you can make sure you are as ready as possible for when the certainty of uncertainty hits you. For example, life is going along swimmingly when, all of a sudden, somebody you love is diagnosed with a terminal illness.

There it comes, like a meteor plummeting down from the heavens above, charging and crashing into your life without notice.

The uncertain becomes certain.

Or you have a dream, a plan to reach a certain goal, and nothing will get in your way, every step has been planned precisely.

Except the unlikely happens, your plans are thwarted and like a thief in the night, your dreams are stolen away leaving you uncertain about the future successes you had dreamed of.

Now I believe there are only two ways to handle uncertainty.

You can be tentative in your everyday living, worrying about 'what might happen' or you can embrace every moment of every day and live in the present, leaving no room for regret. If you can live in the present moment, and accept the passing parade of experiences, it will not only strengthen your will, but strengthen your desire to live a fuller, more enriched life.

This attitude will have you handling yourself much better, under any circumstances. Embrace the uncertainty of your days, be ready to face them with courage and trust by relying on the knowing that lies deep within you. But most of all, trust the process, there is always a Universal reason for every experience in your life.

Unquestionably and without a single shred of doubt, William came into *my* life, and me into *his*, for a reason.

Not that I could have ever dreamed that the final outcome would have been remotely possible.

In the years gone past, I would, from time to time, travel overseas for business. On this occasion I was flying into Jakarta, Indonesia, to meet with a family looking to establish a residence in Australia. There would be an English man to meet, at some point, who was to be the go-between. Arriving at the airport in the early evening, I was expecting the usual maelstrom associated with a busy international airport, so I did not expect to glide through diplomatic avenues without the slightest hold-up. So there I was, five minutes after landing, being ushered into a charming car by an even more charming driver.

What I also wasn't expecting was the crazy traffic, bedlam, near-death experiences, grinding brakes, fearful screeches, and all-out stress; an accurate portrayal of my journey to the hotel. Forget about being in the right lane, you must pretend that traffic lights don't exist, and prepare for beggars to leap out of thin air and hang off the roof of the car; it is all-out war and every man for himself in this city.

My handsome driver, Thomas, a young man in his 20s with a smile as wide as the Grand Canyon, urged me to prepare my mind, body and soul for the endless traffic jams and tragic little beggars that I would experience during my stay. He told me I was safe with him at the wheel and I was inclined to think I would need to feel safe, as my heart was pounding at around 200 beats a minute.

The next morning, I woke to the sound of the phone ringing. It was William and he invited me to lunch at his private club. His driver, Thomas, would be there to collect me at noon sharp, and sharp he was, arriving exactly to the second. If being greeted by William in the carpark was a hint of what was to come, I was in for a wonderful time. The warm timber floors and walls of the dining room, with views towards the gardens, and waiters in crisp white jackets greeted me and made me feel welcome. Everyone acknowledged William as a respected patron, and this was followed by simply outstanding sumptuous food, excellent red wine and silver-service attention. This beautiful environment came a very close second to meeting the very handsome and very personable William Rogers, a consummate professional, and charming and attentive in every detail. The trip was short, sweet and memorable.

But not so memorable that some 10 years later I would still be thinking of William.

After all I had only met him for a total of four hours at the most. So, on a Sunday morning, 10 years on, when I was enjoying the ambiance and leisurely pace of a delicious breakfast with my wonderful husband, the intrusion of the phone ringing didn't take long to shatter the tranquil moment.

The call was from a from a private hospital in the city.

A nursing sister introduced herself as June, and asked if I knew of a William Rogers. I had no recollection of such a person and told her as much.

"That's strange," she remarked. "Your name and phone number is the only contact we found in his wallet."

I did my best to think about the man she was speaking of, attempting to associate the name, when all of a sudden it struck me; of course I knew William, goodness those 10 long years had passed, yet the memory of that charming man came flooding back as strongly as if we had only been dining at that wonderful restaurant the day before.

June asked if I would come immediately to the hospital.

Many years on, people still ask why I dropped everything to go to the bedside of someone I barely knew. At the time, I did not give the situation a second thought, nor would I today.

My husband wasn't quite sure what it was all about, and neither was I for that matter; however, as events unfolded we would not be left with a single shred of doubt.

If first impressions were anything go by then June and I were going to get along just fine. I could see that she was assessing me just as much as I was assessing her. It is generally in the first few minutes of meeting some people that my inner voice tells me to trust them.

She explained how William had been brought to emergency a few days earlier, that he was in a non-communicative state and there was little to do except care for him. June told me that because it was a private hospital the costs were escalating daily at a rapid rate.

She wanted to know if I had contact with his family, and naturally my answer was what you expect, a resounding 'no'.

It was not hard to understand her frustration, because for every avenue she went down attempting to find out more about him, she was met with dead ends. The answers to her dilemma would come a few days later. Meanwhile, June took me to a private consultation room to explain William's illness. At first she had told me it was cancer, but broke down and sobbed and said she needed to tell me the truth.

The doctors had insisted that I not be told of William's real circumstance, but for some reason June felt pushed to tell me how it really was.

William also had AIDS, and this insidious disease had taken a great toll on his body, with the cancer having spread to the spine and brain. She felt so badly for him, and wanted to find his family.

I was her only hope.

I had no idea what I could do about connecting to his family but I knew I could at least bring comfort to the situation by sitting with William.

June did her best to prepare me for what I would see when I went into William's room, and thank goodness I'm rarely disturbed by anything too much.

Poor William's body was swollen up and most of his neck and face was black, his mouth was full of fungal infection that seemed to be multiplying in front of my eyes. June suggested I only speak in soft tones and not touch him as any touch would be excruciating.

"Hello William, it's Elizabeth, remember me I met you in Jakarta?" I whispered gently, leaning over.

He turned his face slightly towards me, and a light shone from his eyes.

"Hello Elizabeth," he said in a very slow, yet relieved way.

June was stunned, these were the first words he had spoken.

I stayed with William for the rest of the day and into the early evening, leaving his bedside only once, going to the hospital shop to buy him a tiny gold guardian angel. I don't know why I felt drawn to do that, but then again nothing was ordinary about the day.

Except for brief moments in time, I continued visiting William, sometimes just sitting by the bedside to provide a comforting presence, other times speaking of anything and everything.

Two days later as I was heading to the hospital, I received a call from a man named Simon. He told me that he was a friend of William's and that he lived in Fiji and owned a marina.

Now I'm sure you are with me by now and would be forgiven for wondering as I did at the time, how he came to have my home number. But as each little bit of the conversation unfolded, William's story was finally coming to light.

William had moved from Jakarta some years earlier and sailed his yacht to Suva in Fiji to retire. His boat was moored at Simon's marina. Some months earlier, William had been feeling unwell and he had decided to fly to Singapore to see his doctor. The doctor recommended he come to Australia to seek specialised treatment, but he had ignored this advice and gone back to his yacht.

Unfortunately, the body, when unwell, has a mind of its own and when matters became worse, he had no alternative but to come to Australia. He had struggled far too long with this illness and pretending it was going to get better on its own was no longer an option. Prior to the emergency arrival at the hospital, he had been staying at a hotel close by and one morning a staff cleaner had found him unconscious. Simon had been trying to get in touch with him for days and when he couldn't, he broke into William's computer on board the yacht and found my details on a friends list. Really! This was becoming stranger by the minute.

He also gave me the contact details of William's brother in the United Kingdom and so it was that a few days later, I was looking after William's brother and his wife.

Michael and Susan were lovely folk but very confused and anxious about everything that was going on. They told me they had arranged for William's parents to fly out from Devon on the next flight and hoped I would stay around to help with what was obviously going to be a very traumatic and difficult time.

Forty-eight hours later, I was caring not only for the matters required in preparation for a funeral and burial, I was looking after a family of four as well.

But, before then, by the time I made it to the hospital the next day, the family had gathered to speak to the doctors. It had been decided not to tell the parents, Kenneth and Rita, about William's real illness, as they were elderly and it did not seem necessary.

Rita asked me to go into the room with her. William appeared quite comfortable, almost as if nothing were wrong. She walked over to him and gave him a soft, gentle kiss on his cheek and said, "Hello Willie, mummy's here now."

A small tear fell down the right-hand side of his cheek and in what must have been the most humungous of efforts, William replied, "Hello mummy, I'm glad you are here, I love you."

Walking out of that room I was barely able to see a foot in front of me for the tears in my eyes.

I would not see William again.

In the early hours of the following morning, Rita felt the urge to go to the hospital and sit with William. Just a few short hours later he drew his last breath. Later Rita told me that at that very moment a red hot air balloon floated past the hospital window.

It was about nine o'clock in the morning, when I was preparing to go in to support the family, that I received the news that William had died. Michael also told me a good friend of William's had just flown in from Singapore and asked if could I come in to meet him and help make the final arrangements for a funeral.

Over lunch I promised to help in any way possible.

I had already called the funeral parlour, a family business that had been going for over 100 years and, best of all, they were good friends of mine, so I knew they would make sure things happened smoothly.

What I had not bargained on was a request for the burial to be at sea. I wanted it to be amazing and special, as this poor family had been through enough.

I did make all that happen. The nurses who had cared for William came to the funeral, the burial at sea was accomplished, we even planted a tree in William's honour.

Finally, after taking this newly acquainted family to dinner on more than one occasion, and a few quite days of reflection, they left Australia to go back to England.

Exactly seven days to the day after that first call from June, we were back to normal.

If you could call it that. How could this have happened after I only met William for a few hours?

Some 12 months later I decided to go to a fantastic spiritual healer, a Dutch woman who I held in high regard.

Before a healing, we always began with her telling me all kinds of things that only I knew of; she would blow my mind each and every visit.

This time it was to be more than that. I was sitting opposite Katrien, when she began talking to the air.

"Just a minute, I'll speak to you in a moment."

With a bothered sigh she told me there was someone there to speak to me and did I know a man called William?

Chills ran up my spine and the hairs on my body stood straight up. I nodded yes and she gave me this message.

"William wants you to know he hated those brown pyjamas they dressed him in. He is also saying that what you did for him and his family will never be forgotten. He is sorry the red wine you had at the club in Jakarta wasn't up to scratch and most of all he wants you to know he will look over you and protect you always as a guardian of the Light."

I just sat there, completely at a loss for words. These were details that Katrien could never have known or even guessed, as I had not been to see her for over two years.

There he was again, the absolutely very personable William Rogers, a consummate professional, charming and attentive in every detail, even in the after-life.

His family had given me a gift before they left, a beautiful sculpture of a woman's head and bust, it is fittingly called 'Woman At Peace'.

I look at her daily, and remember with deep gratitude how the Universe saw fit to bring William and I together to walk a path, one that provided many lessons on a level beyond words, beyond thought and beyond normal understanding.

Out of all the millions of people all over the world, we were destined to meet. I sense William's presence sometimes, especially now, as I write his remarkable story.

Chapter 23
Journey to Another World

"And now we step to the rhythm of miracles from the Light that Never Dies."
Aberjhani

Do you feel you are 'different'?

Do you believe you do not fit in with everyday life?

Sometimes we do feel poles apart from those around us; you'll be relieved to know many people feel this way. We feel this way because it is entirely possible our Soul is simultaneously experiencing an existence in another dimension. This may be a difficult thought for those with particular beliefs; however, through the many regressions I've been privileged to conduct, I know there are people who are living parallel lives.

This story is a surprising revelation and affirms, in my mind, that elementals are real, that they have lived for thousands of years and are still in existence today. It furnishes a wonderful validation for those of you inclined to believe in the realms of fairies and elementals.

Frida is a down-to-earth, strong-minded woman, who I would say is far from being frivolous. She does not believe in God, or spirits of nature, and only gives credence to what she can see and hear.

I have just guided Frida to experience a past life and her voice has changed to a very matter-of-fact style.

"Where are you?" I ask.

"In the water, near the waterfall," Frida replies.

"Is anyone else there with you?"

"My father, he is asking me to come out of the water, but I'm on my way out anyway."

"Does your father have a name?"

"His name is Trimador," she responds without hesitation.

"What are you wearing?" I ask.

"Little bits of cloth, I do have tattoos on my arm though, they are marked as stripes."

Intrigued, I ask why Trimador is waiting for her.

"He is waiting for me because there is much to learn."

"What sort of things does he wish to teach you?"

"Practical magic," she replies.

"Do you live on Earth or another planet?"

"It is on the edge of the Earth."

"So this practical magic your father teaches you, what can you do with that magic?"

"It is just the way our people are."

"But what do you do with that magic?"

"Heal, protect, fly. Everything looks like paint, I touch it and it is wet."

"How long ago is this lifetime?"

"Thousands of years past."

I ask her to go to where she lives and she tells me it is in an old tree. On the way she describes herself to me.

"I'm quite small, I'm little, but I have big feet."

"Are you human?"

She says she is not so I ask if she is an elemental. I think she is unsure of that word, but continues to tell me she is little, so I ask her to explain further.

"I'm the size of a blade of grass, but I have big feet," she goes on. "Ah that's right, that's what the tattoos are. Everyone has a tattoo that shows what their magical talent is. Oh, and by the way, my name is Sharla."

I greet her by her name and ask her to tell me what her magical talent is and she replies that she 'moves earth' so I go on to ask her what she means by that.

"When I touch things they move. I can make them change, it's like paint."

"That sounds so intriguing," I say.

"It is normal to me," she responds.

Sharla has not mentioned her mother and I'm interested to know where she is.

"I do not have a mother."

"How were you created then?"

She does not know the answer to this question, so I encourage her to ask Trimador.

"He says you just become," comes the reply.

"Do you have a Soul?"

"Yes, I do but we are part of nature."

"Do you communicate with Mother Nature?"

"I do because I change things."

"Why do you change things?"

"I do not do it on purpose, we each have things we have to do," she responds with a touch of irritation.

This conversation is so different and I do my best to learn as much as possible about this tiny elemental by asking what she eats.

"I eat berries, leaves, sometimes fish."

"Are you afraid of anything?"

She says there is nothing to be afraid of, so I ask if there are many others like her where she exists and she tells me they are everywhere.

You may well be wondering by now why I have not asked more compelling questions; however, I realise I'm speaking to an energy not of this world, so I do not wish to ask anything that may upset her or have her leave the conversation entirely.

So, weaving my curiosity into the scheme of things must be achieved prudently.

"What does your father do?"

"Well, he is not *my* father, he is the leader, he can do everything, he is everyone's father," she replies.

"How do you get about, Sharla?"

"I fly and I do a lot of walking, that's why I have big feet."

"What happens to your kind when you die, Sharla?"

"We just turn into light."

I'm thrilled to hear this, because throughout all the regressions I have facilitated, the one common denominator related to me at the end of any life span has been for the Soul to go back to the Light, whatever realm or planet they may have existed upon.

"Can you ask your father if he has some advice for the world I come from, please?"

He tells Sharla I already know, so I push her a little further.

"That doesn't help me very much, can he be clearer?"

"The people of your world must treat each other with kindness," she responds.

I ask her if the world she comes from still exits and she tells me that it does. I want to ask about the edge of the Earth, as I'm not sure what she meant.

"Sharla, you spoke earlier about the edge of the Earth. To my mind our Earth is round, so I do not understand what you mean by the edge."

"It is right between the Earth and the universe, it is not hot, it is not cold, there is no danger. We are the connection between Earth and space, we help the world go around," she replies.

I can hardly believe what I'm hearing, and I also cannot doubt the sincerity in which this energy is interpreting back to me the realm she exists in. I feel I'm experiencing a miracle, hearing about the existence of a place in this extraordinary universe, one I could never have believed to be in existence.

The words were flowing from Frida as she lay there so very relaxed.

"Is that your purpose, to help the Earth rotate?"

"No, we are not responsible for the rotation of the Earth, we help the humans. The humans of *your* world do not treat each other with any respect. We keep it together."

I respond by saying that sounds like hard work and ask her if she can go to the last day of that lifetime. We are often unprepared for the answers we receive, as they are not what we expect; Sharla's answer was definitely unexpected.

"I'm still alive. I live on the edge of the Earth."

I tell her I understand this, but that she is communicating with me through Frida in the year 2015.

"I'm aware of that, I'm there and I'm here, I come and I go. She's destined for amazing things, you know."

"Do you mean Frida?"

"Yes, she doesn't think so though, she tells me bad things happen to her one after the other, unfortunately she just has bad luck."

I ask what we can do to help Frida.

"She needs to be supported, she is very blocked at present."

"Sharla, is her son from your world?"

"No, but he is from many different worlds."

I would have loved to ask more about Frida's son, as she had told me in the pre-interview that he has Aspergers, but I realised I might have been overstepping my place. It is essential to know where to draw the line when speaking to someone's Subconscious, as it is a privileged opportunity and something that should never be taken advantage of. I go on to ask about this parallel existence.

"How do you feel about Frida living this life on Earth, Sharla, where would you prefer to be, on the edge of the Earth or part of life itself?"

"I'd rather be Frida experiencing real life, then maybe she would be luckier."

"Who created you and your people, Sharla?"

"The Divine created us to protect the Earth, we just became."

Knowing I could not take Sharla to a last day in her life, because she still existed, I was unsure how to close this conversation, not that I wanted to, there was so much more to learn, but as it turned out, it was Sharla who was to help me.

She must have been reading my thoughts.

"Just do what you have to do, Elizabeth, I will leave when I am ready."

Suddenly Frida sat upright, opened her eyes, then looked at me.

"Just hang on a sec, I need to say goodbye to her or she won't leave," Frida said.

A minute later, she dropped back onto the bed, closed her eyes, and slipped back into the regressed state as if nothing had occurred. Frida had no memory of that moment afterwards.

Over many centuries, fearmongers have portrayed the edge of the world as a place where only evil existed, a no-man's land.

Yet here I was listening to an entity that had invited me past those boundaries, pushing old notions aside, to tell me of a place that had nothing to offer but love and care for our beautiful planet. The whole of the universe, the stars, the planets, and whatever there is in between, is the result of Divine creations, and even if we cannot grasp the concept in its entirety, this discussion with Sharla must at least have cracked open a seed of curiosity within you, over the possibility that such a place on the edge of the world may exist.

Since the beginning of time, disseminators of intimidation have impacted significantly on humanity. When we accept we have the right to our own truth, their stronghold will be weakened, even though they may never want to atone for their ignorance.

It is not for us to judge these disseminators of intimidation either, but if we can collectively draw on the brilliant light of pure love and understanding, and allow this love to run through our hearts and minds, it will awaken us to the understanding that by treating each other equally, there just may be a chance for peace on Earth.

We humans are more alike than un-alike; hopefully one day we will understand this.

Chapter 24
A Mighty Viking Warrior

"Master of magic, god of war, Odin wanders alone."
F.T. McKinstry

Francis arrived at her appointed time, a diminutive woman in stature but with what I recognised to be a sparkling personality, a person impossible not to like.

Knowing that almost anything can happen during regression, I spent a good amount of time getting to know Francis, and it helped me to understand her family history, that she does not believe in God and so on. Knowing how to weave questions into a regression is so important, as these questions bring about a great understanding into our amazing and complex natures.

This experience would prove to be important to her personal growth as she came to understand that she was so much more than what she believed herself to be. Some days are diamonds, some days are gold and this day proved to be both.

"Where are you?" I ask.

"I'm in Scotland," Francis replies.

"Where in Scotland are you?"

"Standing on the mound near the big stone blocks, there's lots of grass around."

Well, I did ask didn't I? It seems my questions will be answered very simply.

I'm curious about the stones, as history tells us there are many interesting groups of rocks that reflect what may have been some form of worshipping culture, and I'm curious to know what they look like.

"They are twice my size and stick out of the ground, some of them have large holes. I do not come from this place, so I do not know what they are."

"How are you dressed?" I ask.

"I'm wearing a kilt of course."

I'm speaking to a man who goes by the name of Hamish, he is in his 20s and has long red hair.

"What are you wearing apart from your kilt, Hamish?"

"Absolutely nothing at all," he responds with genuine humour.

"You mean bare feet, bare chest, nothing under your kilt?"

"That is right"

"Aren't you cold walking around in just a kilt?"

"Yes, but it is invigorating."

"What about jewellery, do you wear any?"

"I wear gold bands on my arms, three on one arm, and one on the other."

"What do the gold bands represent?"

"It is my ranking as a warrior."

"What kind of warrior are you, Hamish?"

"I'm a Viking."

Now I'm excited, knowing there's the likelihood of a side to the life of a Viking ready to unfold. I suggest to Hamish that he go to where he sleeps.

"Yes, I'll walk back down the mound to my ship."

"What does your ship look like, Hamish?"

"Well, its long and narrow and when we travel the seas there is a big sail to help us along. On the front of the ship is a carving of a woman's head, she is covered in gold, but it is only paint though, because she is made from the same timber as the ship. Many men row our ship, they are also Vikings."

"What do you eat on board when you travel, Hamish?"

"Salted raw meat," he replies.

It is such an amazing moment, to observe Francis lying on the bed, speaking as a strong-voiced male, and I'm intrigued as to how Hamish became a Viking.

"I was born into it, my father is the leader, I had no choice."

"Do you have a particular friend on the ship?"

"Yes, I do, her name is Turid."

"There is a woman on your ship?"

"Girls can be Vikings too, you know."

I ask Hamish if he can speak to her, but he tells me she's busy packing because they are getting ready to leave. So I ask what he is doing, and he responds by telling me he is helping as well and they are preparing to push the ship out.

"Have you spoken to Turid yet?"

"She keeps telling me to go away."

Francis begins laughing, she laughs so much, it makes me start laughing, which makes her laugh harder again.

I ask Hamish what he is laughing at.

"I'm drunk," comes his magical reply.

Then he is laughing so hard, it is impossible to go on for the next minute or so. Eventually, I manage to get a word in.

"No wonder Turid is telling you to go away."

Not to be out done he tells me they are all drunk. Attempting to gain composure myself, I decide to ask where they are travelling to, but he has absolutely no idea.

"Anywhere and everywhere, we will travel to rape, to steal gold and take food."

It all sounds very much like a typical Viking life.

"Tell me about a significant day in your life, Hamish?"

"It was the day I told my father I did not want to be a Viking and he became very angry with me." His voice has sobered right down to a grave and almost sad tone. "I just didn't want to be violent anymore, I just wanted to work the land and be at peace, but we live in a time when we have to fight, it is the way of our world. So, I just keep doing what I have to do, go to the ships and work the land. I have nine siblings and they are much younger than myself, so I do all that I can to help my mother."

"Life must be tough for your mother, Hamish."

"Yes, it is, but you live to fight and work the land. That's how it is for all of us. My father and older brother died in battle, so now I have no choice but to keep going."

"Were you sad about that, Hamish, about your father and brother dying?"

"Well, it's sad but it happens all the time, it is the way life is as a Viking."

"What do they do with the bodies?"

"We burn them, if it is one death they float out onto the water burning, if there are many of them, we build up a wooden pile, and inside the pile, we stack the bodies on top of each other and burn them."

"Do your people believe in a God of any kind?"

"Well, yes, we pray to Odin, he is our God of War and Magic."

"Do you believe in magic, Hamish?"

"It depends on the magic. Some women practise black magic, it's dangerous work, they place curses and make people see things that aren't there."

"What about good magic, Hamish?"

"Yes, there is the healing magic, that is the good work, but the healers have to be careful as the black witches do not like them."

Hamish lets out a huge sigh and I ask if he is tiring of our conversation. He tells me he's not but I can hear a real sadness through his voice, a tone of resignation.

"No, I just do not like my life."

"Do you ever find some form of comfort in your life?"

"There is nothing. I just have to get through it."

I take Hamish to the last day of his life. He is dying from old age, and he tells me he did not marry but that Turid is still his woman, and they have five children. His family are waiting outside the home until his death occurs. I want to know how he feels about death and dying.

"I can't wait," he responds.

I chuckle to myself as he says this, because as far as I can see, a tougher life he could not have experienced.

It had been a long hard life, so I encourage this Viking warrior to take his last breath, and be done with it.

Immediately he is in spirit and looking back over his life and I ask him now how old he was when he died.

"I was 109, way too old. But I learnt to accept the things I could not change, I learnt to accept the way life was for a Viking. It was an awful life, but I made the best of what was given to me. I will always care, I have a big heart and I'm hopeful, that is what I want to take with me from that life."

Good heavens, can you imagine living to that age, even in today's time? I think the old adage about 'hard work doesn't hurt anyone' is a most apt one for this old Soul.

"You did a fine job in that life, Hamish, it was tough, but you learned that no matter what was thrown at you, you coped. You will have gained a lot of wisdom from all those experiences. It can be very tough on Earth, and accepting whatever is given to us and dealing with it the best way possible must ultimately be for the advancement of the Soul."

"Yes, you are right, I have gained wisdom. But I hope I do not come back as a Viking next time around."

What could I do but have one last chuckle at this mighty warrior and as I prayed for a less arduous life for that beautiful Soul, I sent Hamish on what would hopefully be a well-earned rest before venturing into his next life.

It seems that Earth, has always been the toughest boot camp in the Universe.

At the moment of death, when the seed atom in the heart is ruptured, which contains all the experience of the past life in a panoramic picture, the spirit leaves its physical body, taking with it the finer bodies.
Max Heindel

Chapter 25
One Tough Boot Camp

"God built lighthouses to see people through storms. Then he built storms to remind people to find a lighthouse."
Shannon L. Alder

I hope I can do justice to Imogen's story; a young woman of immense courage is allowing me to convey her story, one we both hope will bring comfort to all who have suffered a similar fate. This is the story of a Soul who chose to come and teach love to her parents, to break down the barriers of anger, hatred and misplaced love, but sadly her mission would be thwarted by rejection, abandonment and abuse, both physical and mental.

Yet, despite all of this she has drawn from deep within herself compassion and empathy for those who stole her innocence.

Some members of her family are doing life in jail for unforgivable acts against others who were less able to protect themselves.

When once upon a time a younger Imogen would have seen her peers as her allies, her comfort, her protectors, they soon became her arch enemies. Love, compassion and tenderness were influences foreign to this little girl. Having endured beatings, sexual abuse and so much more, Imogen at the tender age of 12, would spend her weekends travelling on trains, day and night, to avoid being the victim to these atrocities.

Just a few months shy of her 13th birthday, she was dropped off at a railway station by her mother and told not to come back home, because she was a waste of her time and energy.

Growing up street smart would become her only option, because as to date her only lessons about life had been on how to self-destruct, lessons that were harsh and imposing. Although petrified of this situation, there was a certain amount of relief and on many levels, it would be a defining time in her life. There was nobody in the family that she could reach out to, they were all perpetrators of murder, rape, paedophilia, mental disorders, you name it, it was rife in that family.

It's hard to imagine that a child could survive, but Imogen has done just that. She is now a young woman with a strong sense of justice, a beautiful Soul who knows what it's like to suffer at the hands of others, and is therefore able to show empathy and compassion to those less fortunate than herself.

I would say her moral compass is in perfect working order.

Imogen came to see me because she wanted advice on how to overcome the effects of harsh judgements from others on her feelings of self-worth.

She wanted to learn how to stop worrying about what others thought, and to stop feeling at fault for everything that went wrong. Life on the streets was severe, but not totally without light.

When speaking of that time in her life, Imogen told me about four homeless men. They were of varying age, a mixed bag of personalities, one with so many tattoos and piercings you could hardly tell who may have existed behind them, yet against all odds she remained safe. It was a very special time for Imogen as these men taught her many of the values she holds close to this day. So there they were; Barry, Moses, Gummy [because he didn't have any teeth] and Snake, her brave knights in shining armour, her saviours. With all this information in hand, I asked Imogen to show me the questions she wanted answered by her Subconscious and with her generous permission here they are for you to see. How do I release myself from burdens to be happy and free? Am I following my destined path? How can I stop taking on other people's emotions? How do I become the great person everyone says I'm going to become? What should I do with my life? How do I start to love myself? Is there anything I need to be aware of? How can I trust myself to make decisions? Why do I not trust people? What is my true life purpose?

Very important questions for this beautiful young woman to ask and discover answers too. Thanks to a series of almost unprecedented opportunities throughout her life, not only was I to learn Imogen had already climbed a mountain of irrefutable barriers, but that she had been able to maintain a permanent defiance against the struggles that existed in her family.

Soon she will be learning how not to take nonsense from anyone and to recognise the shining, brave and beautiful Soul that she is. There are no clever words in this story, and I'd say, given the way in which it unfolds, there will be many opportunities for literary critics to have an opinion on how I've attempted to translate a recording into observations and perceptions.

Nevertheless, this is Imogen's story, spoken through her Subconscious, and is a true and factual account of the rich life experiences that have been her journey to date; an unearthing of advice on how not to allow the past to overshadow her future.

A mother is very important to her child, she is the essence of everything that is loving, she is nurturing a beating heart that is completely dependent on her physically, emotionally and spiritually. Imogen's observations about her early years were mostly about what her mother did, primarily for her own survival, times that rarely included herself. By the age of 8, Imogen had been beaten so regularly, it had become a normal way of life; it was, in her own words 'just part of being a kid'.

Throughout all those early years, she somehow knew that her mother was suffering with her own existence and that Imogen was the outlet for her frustrations. Any parent that rules by force will always succeed in creating a rebellious child.

Imogen did learn how to survive, yet she has never forgotten being abandoned by her mother who, before throwing her out onto the streets, accused her of harbouring misguided thoughts about her current boyfriend, the one Imogen had accused of molesting her. Evidence of these veiled perversities to this day remain in the shadows of darkness, undetected. Yet, this mother is not hated, she is pitied. Imogen has chosen to cast aside the stinging blocks of shame associated with her past, and has come out the other side of it all with a considerable reserve of personal strength, worthy of the strongest combatant. Not everything is visible to the naked eye, especially the multiple layers of veneer we build around our sensitive selves as a protection of sort. But such layers are only ever a temporary fix, a band aid so to speak. Imogen will learn that her powers extend far beyond the physical, that she has a real purpose for being here on Earth, the toughest boot camp in the universe. She will learn that no matter how diverse or tumultuous a life she might be living this time, there is always a definite pattern and reason for connecting one lifetime to another.

Understanding family loyalties will go far beyond the here and now for Imogen, as it is the lifetime leading up to her return in this current lifetime that can be best summarised by the series of events I am about to relate. These events have patiently led her along the path of progress for her spiritual development.

Imogen's human environment has always been in a somewhat devastating state, so it was inevitable that parts of her past she had repressed would continue to raise their ugly heads, and I could only hope my role would be of the greatest value possible to her. There were different facets to Imogen's struggle to seek freedom, and unsuspected and intriguing links were waiting to be discovered that had been quietly biding their time. Dimensions hidden by the charade of excruciating experiences, were torn away to expose a lifetime, so contrary to the one she is living now, that Imogen's sense of identity was finally grounded, leaving her to have the freedom and joy that will connect her distant past to her present awareness.

So, to begin her journey, I guided Imogen to experience a past life. She found herself standing in a marketplace, surrounded by the hustle and bustle of people, the pungent smells of penned animals, and tables piled high with exotic, exquisite fabrics in astounding colours and shades, textured with heavily jewelled stones and braids. She described spices, rugs and dishware, but with a tinge of sadness it seemed to me. When I asked how she was dressed, she said she was covered with a fine fabric over her head, her arms and hands painted in exquisite designs, and with jewels on her toes and ankles, nose and ears.

"Why are you here in this marketplace?" I asked.

"I like to buy fabric and to watch the people enjoying themselves," she replied.

"Why is your face covered, are you a certain religion?"

"No, I hide my face from the people in case I'm recognised.

"What is your name?"

"Arjan," came the reply.

I ask if Arjan will take me to where she lives and she agrees; it is not far and soon after she is standing at the wall of her home, a stone structure that is protecting the people living inside. The entrance is a massive iron and timber gate, and a fierce guard dressed in white pantaloons and shirt, a sabre hanging at his waist, stands by.

Once we are inside, the courtyard, the archways, balconies and doorways appear to be adorned with cream marble ornaments, there are life-sized marble tigers, and fountains and beautiful plants. The descriptions are vivid and easy to imagine. As Arjan walks around inside, I ask who else lives in the house.

"My father," she replied.

"Who is your father?"

"He is the leader, the king and protector of his people."

"Where is he now?"

"He is out hunting," she replied.

"Where is your mother?"

"She died giving birth to me."

"I'm so sorry to hear that. Are you and your father close?"

"Yes, but he is always busy. He has arranged a marriage for me and the time is drawing near."

"How do you feel about that, Arjan?"

"It is my father's will, he has told me I will be happy though, as he has chosen a good, kindly person."

I move Arjan forward to the day of her wedding. It is being held in Arjan's home, and the women dress her in white, with many layers of jewels.

Soon she is walking down a marble staircase towards an unknown future; her father is waiting for her and he is wearing a red turban, with a huge diamond hanging in the centre of his forehead, and a long red coat and pants, his footwear covered in exotic gemstones.

Arjan's face is hidden, as is her future husband's. She tells me she is nervous and does not know the many faces in the hall.

I can see that Imogen is beginning to experience the event in a very up close and personal way, so I assure her we are simply observing a past to understand herself better.

Finally she has the opportunity to look at her husband's face, and she tells me he appears to have kind eyes, and for that she is grateful.

Sadly, it is a loveless marriage.

Arjan goes on to have two daughters, but during that lifetime rarely sees her husband, and at the time of her death, there is no one to be with her apart from her two daughters and the priest.

Her daughters kneel by her bedside and are inconsolable.

I ask where her husband is and it appears he is far too busy to attend to her.

Arjan takes one last difficult breath before succumbing to death.

With guidance from myself, she is able to look down on herself, and she sees an old woman, but she tells me she is not so old, it is the life she has led that has left her looking that way.

The daughters are lovingly bathing the body and dressing it before it is to be placed in a casket covered in jewels. A small velvet bag given to Arjan by her husband on their wedding day is placed on her chest as well as a tapestry covered in Sanskrit that had been made by her daughters. Then a beautiful fabric was laid over her and the casket was closed in preparation for her final journey to be cremated and laid near her father in a temple reserved for them alone.

I asked Arjan how she felt about her death. She was not afraid of dying because she knew she would finally have peace and calm, but at the same she was afraid of leaving her children. I could understand that and told her as much. She then said she felt she was a burden to her husband, for wanting so much of his time.

One of the most important reasons to experience a past life regression is for a person to uncover the rationale behind a chosen lifetime and to realise how the lessons learned from that lifetime, and all our lifetimes, will play such a tremendous role in their current lifetime. These lessons all combine to support our journey towards enlightenment.

I felt humbled as the beautiful Soul Arjan spoke of her purpose and lessons in that lifetime.

"I came into this lifetime to understand that no matter who you are or what you are in society, you can still be a good person and make a difference. I learned that even if you do not receive love you can still give love and teach love. I feel I learned that by being alone so often I understand what it means to be strong under any circumstances and that I must be myself no matter what life had put upon me."

It was a revelation to Imogen; that she had lived such an affluent life and that wealth had not brought happiness as she may have expected it to.

The second past life she experienced was far removed from the first life. In the second lifetime, her name was Annabelle and she lived in a timber cutter's cottage deep in the forest.

Her husband had died in a tragic accident.

She had decided to withdraw from society entirely and simply live out her remaining days in survival mode.

Naturally her day of passing came and went, without anyone knowing she had died. Eventually, her body was found and she was given a simple, yet loving funeral. As she watched that event unfold, she was surprised that people cared. Again, I asked what purpose and lessons were attached to that ordinary life.

"I had that lifetime to remind myself that I did not need others to survive, but in living that life I also learned that it is not always good to be alone, that it would have been better to allow other people into my life. But that lifetime did teach me to stand on my own two feet and to know that whatever happens to me, I will always have the strength to pick myself up and keep going."

In both lifetimes, it was clearly explained that she still has this strength to overcome challenges, and that she has the potential to be mighty and powerful in her current life as Imogen.

It was now time to meet with her Subconscious and to learn what was important for Imogen to know and understand.

"Subconscious, why did you bring forward those particular lifetimes today?"

"To show her she does have the strength, that no matter what happens she can stand tall and move forward on her human learning path. She needs to be strong and understand she is strong enough to do the things she wants to do and not allow her inhibitions to control any outcomes."

"Why did Imogen choose such difficult parents?"

"She chose her parents because she believed she could make a difference, and be the difference in the choices they made."

I spoke to the Subconscious about Imogen's mother, and the anger, the guilt, the absolutely horrendous way in which she had treated Imogen.

"It is Imogen's mother's journey. Rather than acknowledge her own guilt and deal with it she has chosen to not accept responsibility or acknowledge certain incidences, and it has now manifested into hatred of herself. Unfortunately, she has taken this out on her daughter."

"Does she love Imogen?"

"In her own way, and only because she gave birth to her. She does not regret that on one level, but because of the many mother–daughter experiences, hatred has severed the relationship. There is no connection as mother and daughter."

"How can Imogen deal with this now?"

The Subconscious explained that Imogen needed to understand that as a daughter she had done a fine job in trying for so many years to make amends, often apologising for things that were not her fault. Imogen needed to now accept that it's her mother's journey and even though Imogen had given so much love and tried to understand and reason with her mother, the situation cannot be helped.

"It is not her fault," the Subconscious continued.

"Who are you speaking of, Subconscious?"

"The mother, Margaret. When younger, she was a wonderful person, a hard-working, good mother. Her mother, Imogen's grandmother, had a partner who sexually controlled Margaret. Margaret's mother knew this but did nothing about it. When Imogen was born, there was great conflict in the family, because Imogen's father, an uncle to Margaret, was still married to Margaret's mother's sister. Because Margaret was on her own without support, and so completely rejected by the family, she became bitter and twisted. Sadly, Imogen paid the highest of prices for their infidelities."

"Goodness me, Subconscious, how could anyone survive such an appalling upbringing?"

"Imogen has tried to give compassion and understanding, yet she has been wondering of late if she should keep trying or ease back. I have been telling her this for a long time but her will to help and fix is quite strong, even when it has been to her own detriment."

"As you know her father is now in jail. She wants to know why she dived into such a challenging family?"

"I feel Imogen needs to look at her father now as the child and she as his parent. I have instilled into her that he has done the crime and now he is doing the time, which is something that Imogen often quotes herself. It took us a long time to keep her away from the jail, he was emotionally unreachable but again it is his journey. He never sexually harmed Imogen, although there was a lot of physical violence, probably a lot more than she remembers, and she needed protection."

"Who helped protect her, Subconscious?"

"We did."

"Who is we?"

"Myself and the Guides, we understood it was her choice to take this life, but sometimes there needs to be intervention."

I said that I was pleased they had intervened and went on to ask about the grandparents, and was surprised at the response.

"Imogen has always had a relationship with her grandfather. She made a choice not to contact him for quite a few years, but in fact, despite his crimes, he is quite a positive in her life. He is genuinely caring. Out of all the family he is the one with the pure heart for Imogen and her children, he has genuine concern for her welfare."

I ask about the love Imogen's grandmother has for her.

"Her grandmother can be genuine when it suits her, and she carries a lot of guilt for the life her granddaughter had, because she knew she did nothing when that young girl called in the middle of the night crying out for help. She is apologetic now and knows she should have done more and does not agree with how Imogen's parents treated her. It had a significant effect upon the poor child with those detrimental things occurring, especially being cast out from the family home at such a vulnerable age."

Listening to the Subconscious I feel genuine empathy for Imogen and hope with all my heart that the advice she is receiving will benefit her greatly. There is a niggling question in the back of my mind about the four men Imogen had met in her earlier years.

"Subconscious, who were those men Imogen met on the street all those years ago?"

"They were Angels, special Guides selected. They played a great part in protecting Imogen, they had a bigger impact than she realised at the time."

"I had a feeling they were Angels."

My suspicions were confirmed and I felt a joy wash through me.

"We've had Barry make a few appearances in Imogen's life since all that time ago and while I feel she was not quite fond of him, he was a good presence for her. Barry is unaware of his role as an Angel, but he's done many good things for young people on the streets. It shows you humans that a book should never be judged by its cover."

"I suspect you are a thrilled with this opportunity to have your say today, Subconscious."

"I am delighted, it is long overdue. I really need to build her confidence. Build her ability to think about the plans she wants to make and to look at the probable outcomes and say to herself, 'this is what I want, this is what I need'."

"How can you do this, Subconscious?"

"I've been trying a very long time. This is Imogen's life, her journey, her parents are away from her life now, she's grown up, so its okay to make decisions and if mistakes are made then that's okay as well."

"How can Imogen free herself from all these past burdens?"

"By accepting herself and knowing she is in a good place. Imogen has had a lot of support she has been unaware of and even though she has done most of it on her own, we will never let her down. I am aware of a meditation she recently showed to another, one that has helped herself. The one where she walks with a heavy backpack full of worries, worries that are released through intent in the meditation. Imogen really felt she had helped that person to move forward, she also thought she had made a breakthrough for herself. She was correct on both counts.

Then her mother got involved and Imogen went back to square one, and interferences, hiccups and knock backs sent her right back down. Imogen needs to continue on her spiritual path and I would advise her to begin as soon as possible. I remember hearing her thoughts the day she first saw her Guide, yes that's right, she can see Spirit, she was wondering, is this all real? I whispered to her, give it a go, be open minded and embrace it wholeheartedly."

"What path is she meant to be following?"

"She is meant to spread light. She thinks she is here to fix other people's problems, but her real purpose is to spread love, regardless of what a person may have done, where they come from, their walk of life, so to speak. She has extraordinary friends, different people, she never judges and takes genuine joy from giving."

"People tell her she will be great one day, she doesn't know why they say this, would you like to respond?"

"She only need believe in herself, and not take on the opinions of others. Her deep empathy for others allows her energy to leak. She needs to protect herself better. She has the capabilities to be greater, but she is at war with herself most times."

It seems to me that most people are. People that do not love themselves are always at war with having faith in themselves. I ask how Imogen can begin to love herself.

"She needs to respect herself as a person and acknowledge the battles she has overcome, and to be more aware of the triumphs she has had in assisting others and herself. She has a magnificent love for her children, and needs to let go of the scars from the past and realise these scars have not defined her. She is in charge of herself, but I remind her I am always here. This has been her journey, and she took it upon herself to change the journey; in doing so she must learn to trust herself by saying 'I'm responsible for myself'. Imogen has come a long way, she is strong and has learned well, and now it is time to move forward. She is a beautiful Soul. When she accepts herself and sees life as a genuine experience, when she understands that things happen and not to take on board the criticism and opinions of others, she will be truly great."

"Thank you for all the advice you have given to Imogen, I know she will be thrilled and appreciative. I asked her if I could ask you some questions of my own. Do you mind?"

"Go ahead."

"Thank you, Subconscious. I would like to have your opinion on sexual relations and how it affects self-image?"

"Self-worth is tied up with self-image. People do not want to feel rejected, they feel they have to be a certain way to be accepted by others, in whichever combination of sexual partner it may be. Sex is meant to be a really beautiful thing and so it should be. Humans were not given sexual organs and emotions for nothing, but the world has taken it too far and the messages are mixed and confusing. Acceptance is a large part of being human and everybody wants to feel as though they belong.

There are those who will go to any length to gain approval and there are those who prey upon this vulnerability. Look at the fashion of young ones, look at the way alcohol has impacted on people. Look at the way the young now think it is a normal part of life to have sex at such an early age. For most of society, it is no longer an intimate coming together of two beautiful Souls, it is more a desire, often the physical gratification for one and the need of approval for the other. What is left for the young to look forward to as they develop into maturity? It is indeed a sad state of affairs. Fear also plays a part, there is always the 'what ifs'; fears of the unknown forces you humans to do many things that do not serve your Soul's higher purpose.

From a spiritual perspective, we want people to make changes, to follow their gut feelings. Change can be daunting for some people, but without fear, you do not take the chance to change. People need to trust themselves. If they do not land on their feet, then they must pick themselves up and start again. If they do not try, they do not know. Treat sex with respect, think about the beauty of two Souls coming together to express their true feelings in the most romantic of ways. There is so much for the human to learn. I hope this answers your question."

"Yes, thank you, I appreciate your wisdom. I do have another question for you. Does the Divine punish us if we make a bad mistake or do something that is not worthy of approval?"

"If it is at a point where the Divine becomes involved, although we the Guides do the work under guidance, the Divine of course sees everything. Nothing is meant to cause harm and there is no intent to punish. It is always a matter of redirection, helping people to get to the place they need to be."

"Thank you, Subconscious, a very wise answer."

I move on and ask if there are any final words of encouragement for Imogen.

"The best is yet to come for her, there is a bit of work ahead but it is all in her hands, she just has to believe and accept. It is interesting to speak through Imogen to get my message to her clearly, it is a most comfortable experience. She has fought a good fight, but she does not have to do this anymore, the fights are not hers. She has had only 12 lives and they have all been very similar. Mainly she is on this side of the veil.

She is an Angel who put up her hand to try and help us back here have a better understanding. These runs down to your Earth have been most helpful. It is not funny down on your Earth, it is hard work, at least you humans make it hard work, but we understand Imogen is trying her best so we intervene when we need her to.

She is also not the first human I have helped, but I feel lucky to be with her, helping her along her learning path.

Although I'm separate to her Soul, we work closely together to ensure she comes back to the Light safe and sound. It has been a learning curve for all of us and we are very happy."

With that I thanked the Subconscious and the session was completed.

It took some time for Imogen to ingest all this information, but I am pleased to say she has moved forward in her life in leaps and bounds.

Chapter 26
Food For Thought

Questions and Answers from Different Subconscious Energies.

Q:
Does history repeat itself?
A:

Yes, and no, it repeats itself, but not in the same place. Every cultural civilisation goes though the same things.

Q:
What do you think of the world at present?
A:

It is far more complex in all areas. Repetition happens because many people do not have good memories of the past. People have strong ties to past lives, spirituality, all manner of beliefs, but people do not believe enough in themselves, therefore there is a residual effect.

Q:
From where does knowledge stem from in the human?
A:

When one finishes one life and one has learnt from it, this learning builds up like a chapter in a book. The good thing is, as you learn more the book gets fatter. When the book is written like that, you can always read it in the next life.

Q:
Is the meaning of justice what we as humans believe it to be?

A:

Justice is not delivered by the Subconscious. Justice is delivered by an unseen force, it is the world correcting itself. I use the word figuratively as it expands further than that.

Q:
Is justice another word for karma?
A:

It has no name, it is a process, and yes you could call it karma.

Q:
Does justice stem from the Gods, this unseen force you speak of?
A:

This law of justice predates beings like Gods, the 'older ones', because before everything was made, there had to be a law in place first.

Q:
Is that what we call Universal law?
A:

It is more than that, it has always been there. The law was not placed by just one thing. It was a principal before things were made. There are many names to this law and principal.

You may call it karma. It is the principal of what is right and wrong, it is recirculated again and again. It is a process.

It is difficult for humans to learn as it is an old and forgotten notion. This is different from human laws, they are based on history and social understanding. The law I speak of is older than time itself.

Q:
Does this law apply to other planets?

A:

Yes, these ancient codes of conduct apply to all energy.

Q:

What lies in the 80 per cent of the undiscovered parts of the oceans?

A:

Fantastical creatures, people and creatures of your Earth cannot go down there, only the more ancient creatures can survive there. There are creatures there that were around when the world was young, they are more evolved now, but mostly the same.

Q:

Where does the Subconscious go during a general anaesthetic?

A:

It depends. If the person is a higher level of being, the Subconscious will remain in the body. If that person is not of a higher level then the Subconscious moves out from the body. This is because the Subconscious can be hurt and if it can feel pain, it will be harder for them to make proper decisions.

Q:

Ok, so if the Subconscious removes itself from the body where does it go?

A:

It hovers above the body or stays in a corner of the room observing.

Q:

If the body dies on the operating table, is it because that person was meant to die at that given moment in time?

A:

No, the body can die when it is not meant to. Because what you all call God can come and end that life because there is something better that can come about.

Q:

If this energy we do call God comes in either to save or take that Soul back to the source, is this some kind of contract?

A:

Yes, they are special consecrations.

Q:

Do mermaids still exist?

A:

Yes, but they are reclusive Souls, they do not live in all areas of the ocean anymore, they only live in the deepest darkest depths, the place they have always lived.

Q:

I thought they were happy creatures?

A:

They are happy, but they can be territorial. They are tough, not like your Disney film characters. They are fighters, but do not feel sorry for them, they always find a way.

Q:

Were the mermaids created on purpose or by accident?

A:

Yes, and no, they were put there for a purpose, but they were not supposed to be mermaids, that simply happened by accident.

Q:

Were they meant to be half human, half fish?

A:

I cannot reveal that, but if you are truly curious you can find this out from your own Spiritual Guidance, and if you do find the answer it will be extremely interesting.

A colleague was observing this regression and without missing a beat she asked if it was meant to be a swordfish. The room filled with laughter as the Subconscious replied:

A:

I like her she is good and she is right. They were not from man, they were what man was supposed to be, a being living amongst animals. But man became land dwellers, they were originally from the ocean.

Q:

They were swordfish?

A:

The ones you know as people today were not the first, mermaids were. That is why there is the saying 'all things come from the ocean'.

Q:

What about the evolution of the ape?

A:

All things came from the ocean. Man came from fish to the Earth. The ape was a form of jellyfish, they were much bigger and had more limbs. When they came to the land they developed hair. If you had to imagine something, imagine an ape with fins and a jelly-like body, that is what they were.

In closing this chapter, I would like to acknowledge the Subconscious minds that brought forth the information.

It has been written exactly as it was recorded and is obviously going to raise a few eyebrows, but for me, this is the joy of regression; the conscious mind, that ego mind, is well and truly out of the way.

Part 3

Important Questions about Life

"I never dream to become someone important for myself. The truth is that I really don't have a personal ambition. My ambition, my dream, it's about the people. It's all about the people. It's for the people. It's all for the people. That is my ultimate goal."

Nurudeen Ushawu

Chapter 27
Leaves of Light

"Remember the clear light, the pure clear white light from which everything in the universe comes, to which everything in the universe returns; the original nature of your own mind. The natural state of the universe. Let go into the clear light, trust it, merge with it. It is your own true nature, it is home."

The Tibetan Book of the Dead

My spiritual growth has always come from asking for guidance and this has led to me trusting myself when connecting with the Universe. We all have spiritual helpers ready to advise when we ask. Coping with life can be challenging for the best of us, so I set out to discover the best advice possible regarding the journey of the Soul.

I met Childrahan by asking for a Guide to bring a wisdom worthy of sharing with the world.

The connection was immediate.

Thankfully, I was using the art of Automatic Writing. Maybe you have not heard of this way in which one can connect to Spirit? Automatic writing is a form of channelling, and requires allowing yourself to stand aside and enable words to flow through you.

It is a very effective way to channel Spirit, and probably the easiest type of communication with Spirit to learn.

It is a gift that we all have.

Drawing on the energy I felt enveloping me, I began to write.

"I am Childrahan, Guardian of this light source, Keeper of the Key to the understanding of the Soul Journey from its beginning.

All energy begins at the source, whatever this energy may be. The Soul is the same.

Even the most wayward of Souls had a beginning and it was from the same source as all others. So, where is this source I speak of? Far away from planet Earth there still exists a place and time that has never changed or evolved.

For this is where Souls are created, before being chosen to move into a life form. As you are aware, there are many life forms, from plants to animals, humans and many other forms in-between. Anything that has energy has a Soul.

You humans believe you are the only ones who have a Soul and you are wrong, for apart from all human energy, there are millions and millions of other forms of existence with the same Soul matter, you are a minute part of a very big whole. This does not make you unimportant, for indeed you are all very important."

"Why is this so, Childrahan?" I asked out aloud.

"Because you have been given a life form that allows you to seek knowledge and adventure in relative safety. Not all parts of the whole of the Universe are safe, no far from it.

You think that the wars upon your Earth are cruel and ugly to you and yes, they are and to the Divine Creator of all things this is so. However, having said that, there are far more challenging places to be.

You might see Earth as a fantasy land, for indeed it is a very beautiful place. Your Souls reside in a human vessel so that you may enjoy the fruits of the land. It is a magnificent planet. I come with these words of wisdom so that the people of the Earth find reason to celebrate their existence. Allow me to explain.

When the Soul is created and it is planned that they should have their first experience of many upon Earth, they are provided with all the attributes that will lead to a full and successful existence.

There is also the gift of free will, this is stored into the vibrations of each Soul, for to seek enlightenment, each Soul must face challenges to grow. It is important that the Light source is kept alive with the energy of pure love. To do this, it must bring constantly to its centre the purest forms of unconditional loving energy, this is how it survives.

Of course, there are those who have sought to oppose this Light, to bring darkness to the Light.

This is why we give Souls, lifetime after lifetime, the chance to cleanse themselves of free-will actions and to come back to the core centre where their Soul truly belongs.

It is a simple process.

The whole matter of having lifetime after lifetime is very complicated and far too difficult to lay before the human mind to absorb. The one thing that is easy to understand, is that goodness can only came from goodness. That every Soul in human form has only one task, and that is to live a life of love and truth."

"It is said that Jesus came and died, and rose again and would that be true, Childrahan?"

"He does exist in Spirit form, he also walks your planet today, doing what he did all that time ago, bringing peace, teaching peace and spreading the word of Love.

The Soul is given many journeys to experience, each one laced with the promise of growth, an understanding of that which it needs to accomplish enlightenment. The journey for humans is a complex web, with many paths and multiple experiences to be had, and this journey is always drawing the Soul towards a wisdom that satisfies its need.

You people become so concerned with the small everyday worries and these small worries are holding you back from the true purpose of your lives.

Do you think that your Soul wants you to experience worry and judgement on every path you wander upon? No, it is asking you to recognise the opportunity to grow forward. Do you think that it is the desire of the Soul to interfere in other Soul lives?

No, it is not.

So you see, each of your Souls is on its own journey to seek the truth of its reality. For so it is, that each Soul has its own reality to seek answers about.

This does not mean you are not here to help one another.

What it does mean is that each of you is full of wisdom, full of knowledge of all that there is; however, you are not aware of this consciously, because you are here to learn. Unfortunately, you continue to seek gratification from the material world and this is a world that carries little wisdom.

This is your greatest test, the material world I speak of.

You are to test the free-will gift you have been given in each reincarnation.

This free will tests your discrimination, to see if you can observe and divide the realness from the illusion.

It is only an illusion, your material world, like a magician may create as a trick at the Circus.

It is time to set aside the 'needs' that you think are so important to your existence and look into yourself to seek the answers. There is no one else that can do this for you, other than yourselves, as you seek the answer to peace and harmony, love and truth. Bringing this thought into the light will help you to see more clearly what your true purpose is.

Do you believe that this wisdom that lies within you is not to help your fellow man? This is the true purpose of the human journey, the human's existence.

To be of service to your fellow man. A life of waste will deplete the energy within; the Soul requires love, it requires feeding, just as your physical body does.

What happens if you do not look after your physical body? It becomes ill does it not? Your Soul is no different, it requires the same amount of care, if not more so, than your carcass.

Why is this so, you may ask?

Because dear friends of the Earth, your Soul is immortal yet fragile. It needs to be tended to with care, it will never die, but will continue on its path despite your human self.

So, when you feel too tired, when you feel you do not have an ounce of strength left to do anything, it is your Soul that is tired. It is tired of not being recognised.

What happens is that it cannot move forward on its journey to enlightenment without learning lessons. This is why you are in this human carcass, to give your Soul the chance for further growth. Becoming aware of this thought will lead you to having the life you are meant to live, one of joy and happiness, one of love and contentment, one of helping your fellow man.

There are many places other than your Earth, places where only hate and war exist, and there are also beautiful places for Souls who have graduated from your Earth-plane school and now reside there, enjoying the fruits of their labour, a place where they enjoy a natural state of peace and harmony.

So dear friends, it is now a time when you have clearly been given an opportunity to step up to the plate, a saying you have on planet Earth, I believe.

Those of you who sense these words as coming from a source of light that is all loving, brought to you with love and truth, will recognise them for that they are.

You will begin seeking your own truth, your own reality.

For those of you who choose to do this, life will begin to feel fulfilled and worthwhile. For those of you who are not ready to accept these words as truth, do not concern yourselves, for when you are ready, when you know in your hearts that these words you have read have merit, then the switch will flicker on and you will see the truth as it is.

I thank you for your assistance in writing my words dear Elspeth, and I thank the reader for their valuable time in reading these words I have spoken."

You are always in my Light
The Light of Truth and Love
Childrahan
Keeper of the Secret of Souls

Chapter 28
Impaired Integrity

"Life is neither good or evil but only a place for good and evil."
Marcus Aurelius

I wonder if the architects of Rome's foundations understood that it was to become one of the world's most powerful civilisations?

The emperor Marcus Aurelius, who even in the midst of all conflict, practised meditation as a source of guidance and inspiration in order to better protect the citizens of his country. On the other hand, nearly 100 years earlier, Nero's brutal campaign to impose violence and corruption would undermine every fibre of moral integrity. His modus operandi? To destroy the touchstone of love and faith of the human race. Before taking his own life, this despot concentrated his full attention to the subjugation of Jerusalem, a tragedy of gigantic proportions.

There is so much evil in the world today, so much unnecessary destruction, so I set out to understand why the human race has not learned lessons from the past and why people still need to kill and wreak havoc.

As long as humankind has existed, there has been a thorn in the side of moral integrity.

Joseph, a man of goodness, agreed to be regressed thereby affording me the opportunity to ask about this very real situation our world is still dealing with.

"It is the breeding, the Romans had a strong bloodline, today that same bloodline runs through those who continue to believe in their own corruptive powers. These people who have self-indulgence are not good people, and you see it everywhere in your world today."

I asked this wise Subconscious about acts of violence.

"Remind society that people must change, as many are driven by self-indulgence. Thousands of years ago, men kept slaves, treated their women and children badly, destroyed anyone and anything that had less than them. Breeding, it's all about the breeding and bloodline."

Still, to this day, there are countries experiencing death and destruction, with despots intent on dictating the behaviours and beliefs of their people, at a level that could easily be likened to the Roman days of devastation. So again, I ask why?

"It is pure evil. Unfortunately, we have to have evil in the world, see it as yin and yang. I do not believe in what they do at all, but everything cannot be good all the time, just as everything cannot be bad all of the time."

"Subconscious, the devastations and disasters experienced around our world, are they some sort of punishment from the Divine for the immorality we continue to impose upon each other, or is it just bad luck or is it created?"

"No, that is created. People continue to overbreed. I do not believe in killing humans, nonetheless as an example, perhaps you could look at countries involved in terrorism. Thousands of children are bred, they come straight from school with a gun in their hand. You know you have to wipe things out like that to a degree, you have to cleanse the Earth sometimes."

I speak of the floods and famine that plague our planet.

"We are extremely overpopulated on this planet, and there are Souls that die because of this, some of them die from personal choice, others, well for them, the choice is made on their behalf," the Subconscious says.

"Who makes those choices?"

"God does. People live longer these days, the poor do not have homes to live in, governments put the prices up, they do not accommodate the needs of the everyday citizen, and that is difficult. It is tough on your planet."

"When people pray to God the Divine and the Archangels for help, do they hear them and help them?"

"They do hear them, very clearly, and they help in a way. They guide, they make people aware of their own choices, they help shine a light on the left and the right side of the road, though the people will always have free will. They need to learn in order to earn."

There has to be truth in this because the many Subconscious minds I've had the pleasure of speaking to have repeated the same mantra, we learn to earn. Fear is also a big thing for us, not the fight-or-flight kind; but, for example, the fears that derive from worrying about death, pain, fear of life itself and the deprivation of liberty.

"It is a necessary part of life. Going back to the Romans, the terrorists of their day, they all felt fear, it may be hard to believe, but they were still human. To a degree, the problem is they do not feel enough fear. It is important for the good people in life to feel fear, and not to be afraid to feel it, it is healthy and it balances your life. Unfortunately some people suffer more than others. Sadly, there are doctors out there who throw medication at these fears and phobias, the fears that create enormous anxiety. It is all about love and understanding, the people of your world need to improve their listening skills."

The major part of my work is in helping people overcome their greatest fears and guilt, so I decide to ask the Subconscious what it thinks about the value of regressing to find answers.

"It is a release, it is informative, you might say it is almost like purging lifetimes, purging good and bad experiences, it enlightens the *self*."

"What advice can you provide to the people of the world, so they can feel more secure?"

"Listen to themselves, they need to listen to the intuitiveness that is built into their psyche. The evil people ignore it and make the wrong decisions. The good people ignore it and often make wrong decisions as well. You know it is all about going with that gut feeling and that is the truth of it all. People know it before they have even thought of it."

"Do you have any advice for the wrongdoers of our planet, something that gives the good people a glimmer of hope?"

"There is nothing. They are evil, and they are never going to go away; and, unfortunately, they are a necessary evil. We do not like it of course, but some people are just born dishonourable. I go back to the ancient Romans, it is the bloodline again, it is bred into them. Having said that, they may not always be born into that kind of life, but they might not have a choice either. The dark nature of a lineage can have some poor Soul forced by their situation, believing that their manner of living is the only way forward. This is a hard one for those people to draw away from."

Despite the herculean task we have ahead of us on planet Earth, my hope is that the adversities, corruption and oppression we still suffer today will in time be replaced by tolerance, acceptance and unconditional love.

Chapter 29
Till Death Do You Part

"It is divinity that shapes, not only your ends, but also your acts, your words and thoughts."
Swami Sivananda

I promise to be true in good times and in bad, in sickness and in health. I will love you and honour you all the days of my life.

That's a pretty big promise to make not only by way of a wedding vow, but to the Divine Father before our entry to Earth.

Coming down to planet Earth for a visit, whether it be for a few hours or a hundred years, we have made a real plan. We *have* the knowledge within to live an abundant and purposeful life.

But what gets in the way of being human? Well, in a nutshell, we do. It is far from an easy ride; but no matter how we choose to live our lives, we will always be governed by that untouchable, unseen, Universal energy that appears to always right the wrong.

My Guides have told me this Earthly life is the toughest one.

How often do we jump into making decisions without thought?

We require discipline, fortitude and self-belief.

There is no magic recipe to leading the perfect life, but when we look at individuals with the great success stories, it seems they are always people who have passion and who have learned to believe in themselves.

The biggest challenge we face is convincing ourselves we are worthy of being accepted for who we are.

A long time ago, there lived a young man whose name was Chiron. He was known as the eldest and wisest of the Centaurs. One day he was badly wounded by an arrow that had been dipped in poison, and no matter what he did to help restore his own health, the wound would not heal. Chiron could not understand this because he believed himself to be immortal. He continued to suffer immeasurable pain, to the point that he withdrew himself from his people to live in solitude and misery. It was not until he had fallen into a pit of absolute desperation that he was forced to leave his grotto to forage for something to relieve the pain.

His search led him to discover the power of plants and herbs and how they could heal. During his meanderings, he met many mortals who also complained of pains and suffering. The kind-hearted side of his true self emerged and led him to become a wonderful healer.

He was known as the 'wounded healer' and after his death it is said that Zeus immortalised Chiron as a star, adding his sparkling light to the Centaurus Constellation.

That star twinkles in the universe for all the world to see and to remind us that courage, compassion, love and healing are the only answers when searching for self-worth and unconditional love for one another.

The story of Chiron rests solidly in the annals of history as a Greek myth. Plato, the Greek philosopher, remarked that this story had a considerable amount of fiction attached to it, yet the Greeks generally viewed the story with great respect and as an honest account. Who are we to argue with what may or may not have happened, the moral of the story rings as true today as it did way back then.

And the moral is: all humans have the potential to be extraordinary even in the most challenging of times.

When we begin to think of ourselves standing as one, on a global platform, committed to working smartly on how we can help one another to alleviate pain and suffering, hunger and poverty, and taking actions that will help sustain human progress, then we will have made the sacrifices our predecessors went through for our mutual benefit. It will be worth the effort. Till death us do part, we have the chance to make a real difference to life on planet Earth.

Chapter 30

Regardless of What Matters to God

"God's definition of what matters is pretty straightforward. He measures our lives by how we love."
Francis Chan, *Crazy Love: Overwhelmed by a Relentless God*

Why are there so many temptations on Earth, the ones that appear to adroitly turn us away from living a peaceful existence?

It's my belief that they materialise in our lives for the purpose of teaching us lessons. Many temptations are designed to test our resistance; in other words, to throw our moral compass off course. I also believe we are deliberately distracted, through free will, in order to experience the difference between right and wrong.

These tests are intended to play a vital role in the development of our life skills. They might be seen as the trade-offs that were necessary to provide a more worldly education, by helping us to evolve individually, to acquire the ability to identify, figure out and handle more easily the stressful situations we come across day after day.

Formidable burdens are part of the serious business of being human, whether we accept that to be a truth or not. There is always a purpose behind every adversity and when we can recognise this purpose, I believe we can learn the fundamental difference between prudence and recklessness.

Whatever way we choose to approach life, there will always be an opportunity to learn. How tough life becomes depends entirely on the approach we have chosen to take.

Nobody is any better than another, we are all equal and as mentioned earlier, we have all had to experience every facet of being human, the good, the bad and everything in-between.

It is written in Matthew 7:1-3

Judge not, that ye be not judged.

For with what judgement ye judge, ye shall be judged and with what measure ye meter, it shall be measured to you again.

It is possible that not everything written in the Bible is the truth; after all, it was written by the hand of man, however to judge another while not being beyond reproach ourselves is, in my opinion, tempting fate. What matters most is that we keep trying, that we do not give up on ourselves. We are loved unconditionally, regardless of what we may have said or done, and of that there is no doubt.

Every human on Earth has underlying issues or unresolved hurts.

If it is not something that affects them due to their current action in their current lifetime, then you can be sure these issues and hurts will be from a past life. So, it is natural to be sensitive to criticism; after all, we will react to anything that causes heartache and pain, won't we?

Often what can appear to be a calamity to us can in fact be the end of a huge lesson, we just have to hang in there long enough to get through to the other side. It is like coming up against two mighty warriors, coexisting within ourselves, battling against one another to see who will win the war. If you want a positive conclusion to any outcome, then you will have no choice but to bring new energy to your challenges and to not feed those existing fears and phobias.

Regardless of what matters to God, the Divine, more importantly it is what matters to us as individuals, as a Spiritual Soul, on this human journey.

This is our pilgrimage, our truth, our opportunity to grow.

Temptations will be thrown at us every day and they will *always be hard to resist,* especially the inclination to exercise that part of our ego, the one that agrees with anything you want it to believe. It is a part of our mind that is strong and forceful. Imagine those pesky weeds that grow in your garden, you can dig them out as much as you like, but if you don't get that root out then they just keep growing back. Ego is no different. You have to find the root cause of temptation and dig it out.

The sum of all our fears will invariably draw us towards sobering and complex misunderstandings, and blind us to the flawless and magical mysteries of life, to the miracles of Mother Earth herself, who holds her rightful place within this infinite universe where the footprint of man's existence is but a mere blimp.

Yet, despite everything, we continue to be safe and loved unconditionally by the Divine. There isn't a religion or political power existing in the world that can control the powerful rotation of Earth, that unseen force allowing our planet to spin safely.

To see her bathed in sunlight during the day and graced by the moonlight at night, the oceans and rivers and soils providing nourishment to sustain our existence, is a miracle.

Mother Earth is a power unto herself, and she has no adversaries, but should the people who scar this planet be blinded to this power, then they will be in for a mighty shock, because it is in those unpredictable, unforeseen moments that reality can strike forcibly and without warning, as a reminder that we are all susceptible to experiencing loss, feeling pain and shedding tears.

Love is at the heart of all matters.

Chapter 31
A Letter From My Father

"We can believe what we choose.
We are answerable for what we choose to believe."
John Henry Newman

On 3 September 1939, the then Prime Minister of Australia Robert Menzies announced Australia's involvement in the Second World War. In the early 1940s, my father lined up with fellow Australians to fight for his country's freedom. He was 21 years old.

The impact of war can do many thing to a person's mind.

Now, some 77 years later, we are at war again.

This time a more sophisticated war, because we cannot always tell who the enemy are and when they will attack.

Sadly, terror cells are constantly active throughout the world and there is a merciless war against terrorism.

No longer is it safe to simply travel, go about our business, take a holiday. Security is a huge thing, inciting within us fears we have never known, making it difficult for some of us to feel safe.

My father was shot twice and suffered constant ill health after coming home from the war. During that mad war time of destruction in New Guinea, he watched as friends were blown apart and lived in constant fear and terror of death.

While in another part of the world, his brother, Eric, was captured and forced to work on the Burma Railway and soon after Eric was imprisoned at Changi prison. This is enough, in my opinion, to make any man bitter and damaged.

Neither of them ever were.

My father proved that you can't do much about war as an individual, but you can change the way in which you choose to live with the consequences and aftermath.

Yes, we do live on a tough planet, but at the same time we can choose how we live, despite any challenges we may face.

The Gilbert River runs a 610-kilometre course and is located west of Georgetown and Croydon in Queensland, Australia. The river was named in 1845 in honour of the naturalist John Gilbert, who was killed in an engagement with an Aboriginal group on the coastline of the Gulf of Carpentaria.

After the war, Dad came back and married his sweetheart Thelma. In 1949, having had their first child, they travelled 1647 kilometres in an old Chevrolet to the Gilbert River to make their fortune in gold. Eventually, the time came to travel back to Brisbane and make a fair living, especially since Mum was pregnant with me.

Some 48 years later at the ages of 78 and 79, and pulling an old caravan that they had refurbished, Dad and Mum prepared to make one final trip to the Gilbert River.

During that time I received my last ever letter from Dad. It is a document of great importance, not only for my family, but for every human to read. It is a fine example of appreciating the simple things in life and how we can change the way we choose to see the world we live in. Both my father and Uncle Eric were consummate examples of mind over matter.

Town Common, Gilberton
Population 9 (including Mum and Dad)

18-12-97

5.15 am

Our darling daughter,

Firstly, we hope you and the family have a wonderful Christmas and find time to relax. We have the little tree and decorations you sent sitting on the camp table. Our Christmas Day menu sounds good, ham, chicken, fruit freeze and white wine, wow!

We had a BIG storm, two and a half inches in an hour, I got out all the water containers together while Gods' precious rainwater filled them to the brim, even the frogs started up.

The River is brown owing to the run off. I've just been for a skinny dip, it is so refreshing, no crocs [crocodiles] today!

The country is looking terrific, green grass everywhere, there's a big wild bull around our place, nearly knocked the outdoor shower over this morning so I had to put a few more pegs in the ground, can't have Mum exposed if you know what I mean.

But he is as gentle as a lamb and I call him 'Lawnmower' because he keeps the grass low for me. Went to the gully earlier, got a bit of gold, enough to fill a tooth. Mum's been terrific, puts up with roughing it, but our togetherness is great. She looks forward to letters, got a bundle yesterday from family. Its bloody hot up here today 42 degrees, too hot to visit the gullies, so we are resting, playing scrabble and having a very cold beer (nectar of the Gods I reckon). We get it delivered by the mailman from the Einasleigh Pub 120 kilometres away.

Not expecting any visitors, in fact no-one has passed for a month. Went on a bit of a walk a few days back, saw plenty of Kangaroos, Galahs, Plains Turkeys, few Joe

Blakes [Australian slang for snakes]. Lots of magnificent trees, the air is so clean and fresh, hard to get sick here.

Loved your recent letters, our Elizabeth, full steam ahead, throwing the past away, just like I did after coming back from war.

There are so many wonderful moments to have in the future, the joy of just being alive, to see and experience basic things, nice things, the soft touch of a warm hand, real smiles, the feeling of inner happiness to share with each other and the world.

Every human must reach the stage where they do not require much, its true we all like to have special things around us, and many of them hold memories from one experience or another, and if we use our minds to deliberate on those positive things, then real magic can occur. Laughter is so important, a release without trying.

Ask yourself 'When did I really laugh last?' you may be surprised at your answer.

I haven't been getting much gold lately, these gullies have been mined and prospected for more than a hundred years, first by the Chinese, think they wiped us clean out of gold, because there is not much left, not that I can find anyway.

But we love to poke about, no one to worry us, no traffic, no noise, just the beautiful birds endlessly supplying their beautiful musical notes.

Mother Nature has hidden her gold for millions of years and if she chooses for us to find some then we know we are meant to have it. Who knows!

It is 2.30 in the afternoon now and nearly brew time, then a spot of fishing for tonight's dinner, Black Bream cooked over hot coals makes a fine meal.

The flying doctor lands sometime tomorrow, need a few pills.

Think my heart is still ticking, hang I'll check, yep the old ticker is still pumping, it is a bit tired though.

The frogs have stopped, they know a thing or two.

It's three days later now love, taking my time to write to you, aren't I?

It's a beautiful morning, a red sunrise, I went out and only got a few specs, before my eyes that is! Mum made some apricot jam from the dried fruit you sent, looking forward to that on some toast.

I'm sitting at our camp table looking out at the river, the beautiful trees, hearing the birds sing. The contrast of the red soil, the green of the new grass and the silver leaf ironbark give a great concept of the Aussie wilderness, or the outback as it is called, it's all a far cry from the war, you would love it darling daughter.

No work today though, its mail day, always great for the mob, the nine of us get together and yarn, talk about Red Rock, Gum Flats, Split Rock, The Granite, The Eight Mile, The Hogan. Funny hey? All the places we go panning for gold.

Anyway the mailman dumps the mail bag down, and while Mrs Michelmore, she's almost 100 years old now, makes a cup of tea.

Dave the local hermit, sorts the contents.

Funny to hear his remarks:

"Gawd, look how long that letter has taken." or "Who wants another bill?"

Anyway back to a bit of advice love.

Problems haunt many people, it is a fact, I have seen it throughout my life. How do I handle them?

Well, if I can't do much about things, I discard them. I think positive thoughts, I always throw away things I cannot change. It is the future that needs the effort, we need to dig deep and find inner strength, roll up the sleeves so to speak and start each day as a new adventure.

It is no point in crying over things that cannot be regained.

Every day people should smile at themselves in the mirror, set their minds in a positive frame and get into whatever it is that needs doing. My darling daughter, I could hug you to death I love you so much.

I have a thing to say about family as well, perhaps you could pass it on one day. Family: No matter who you are.

The true bond, the loving bond, regardless of time, joy, sadness, sorrow, whatever, that bond is made stronger by concern, compassion, love, honesty and trust with each other.

None of us escape from memories, flashbacks I call them, some good and bad, others indifferent, mostly good. Thoughts which bring a laugh or a tear, it is the past that mainly concerns people and it shouldn't, it is the future that's important, the things to look forward to, the happy times, all of which need nurturing as they come along. The most important thing I have learnt in my lifetime is when one loses a family member. Immediately our thoughts turn to, I wish I had been closer, I wish I had shown more love, all those regrets.

My hope is for the people of the world not to wait till it's too late, to show love for each other, to genuinely act out of concern for family members, hug them, provide the warmth of friendship, forget and forgive the past, be themselves, show compassion, bestow unconditional love and finally to pass these attributes on as if they were the most precious jewels in the world.

Lots of love

Your Dad xx

My father died a few years later, the heart finally giving in.

Dad's ashes were taken back by my wonderful brother and his two sons to be buried under his favourite gum tree. A brass plaque was placed as a reminder of the amazing man that never allowed the negatives of life to take control over his happiness.

A powerful lesson to understand and apply to our own lives.

Earth isn't just a planet, it is a boundless energy, it places the condition of acceptance upon us to be the best we can be.

To show no bitterness or regrets.

To grow through our mistakes. To let ego go, and just be.

Multiple generations have struggled through slavery, racism, bigotry, poverty, famine, cruelty and war, but at the end of the day it all boils down to one thing; to be grateful for breath and every good experience that comes your way.

The rest is up to us as individuals, doing what is necessary to be the best we can be.

Chapter 32
The Nature of it All

"Sometimes I think we're alone. Sometimes I think we're not. In either case, the thought is staggering."
Buckminster Fuller

Buckminster Fuller was one of the most fascinating and original minds of his century. Buckminster was born in 1895 in Massachusetts, USA. He believed that divinity pervaded all of nature, and he rejected the established religious and political notions of his time and he reminds me so much of my Spiritual Guide Amon. He said that 99 per cent of who we are is invisible and untouchable, and I wholeheartedly agree.

This chapter is about advice gathered from the many Subconscious minds I've had the privilege to meet. There is a part of ourselves that we tend to feed on a regular basis, and that is the all-powerful, crucifying ego. It likes the attention, feeding off the constant mind chatter, especially the negative thoughts it soaks up like a super sponge.

The higher-self is hard pressed to get a word in edgewise, but if you can learn to distinguish the difference between the ego and higher-self and train your heart to remain open, then you'll definitely change for the better. A human being cannot sustain itself without the essence of spirituality, because we are spiritual beings in a temporary vessel. The ultimate objective for our time on Earth is to experience the contrast of different lessons in each of the lifetimes we come here to live.

The role of Past Life Regression Hypnotherapists is to help people understand the nature of their unique journey.

Past Life Regression Hypnotherapy can change your life, because the all-loving Subconscious is your life partner. It knows you inside and out, and has access to every single occurrence that has ever taken place to you throughout every lifetime you have had.

It understands how your personality was shaped, its intelligence is fundamental and the knowledge you can gain from it is so much more than any university of learning can provide, or anything else for that matter, because nobody knows you better than yourself. Believe it or not!

We as a human race have been defined by impulse, subjugation and confrontation so when it comes to standing up for ourselves, it can be challenging because we've been pushed, shoved, hung, drawn and quartered for millennia in our endeavour to live peacefully. Despondency and dependency have been the flagstones of victory for many an oppressor, and these dictators have been a central repressing force in many countries.

So, it is no surprise that after being thrust up against those walls of tyranny and negativity, we continue to search for who we are and what we stand for.

Past Life Regression Hypnotherapy is not something formidable, you do not lose control over your ability to know what is happening. In fact, it is quite the opposite, you learn everything about who you are and what you are capable of.

There is an instinct in all of us that knows intuitively that there's more to our existence than just eating, working and sleeping. It is an outright miracle that we've had wonderful pioneers, extraordinary people who set out to learn through trial and error the workings of the human mind, inspiring and teaching others and, despite the risk of ridicule by cynics, they forged on regardless.

Undeniably, there was a purpose for their Soul's journey, which was to bring clarity to our struggle for acceptance as a citizen of planet Earth. Whatever would we have been like without them?

The notion that a Past Life Regression provides the best evidence of a person's identity is defined by the intellect of the all-knowing Subconscious, the supreme commander of our self, who demonstrates, time after time, a considerable awareness of all that is. No matter how someone might attempt to divert us from our Soul's journey, or to rearrange our unique make-up, they will fail. There is not a religion, war or punishment that is able to obstruct the journey of the Soul, not even death can erase that because the Soul is untouchable. The Subconscious is the first and last bastion for the Soul's survival, the Divine Spirit took care of that a long time ago, so our fear of fear can only survive if it is fed, otherwise it does not exist.

Thanks to the many who have walked before me in this field of work; wonderful Souls such as Franz Anton Mesmer, Milton H. Erickson, Dr James Braid, Dr Sigmund Freud, Dr Brian Weiss, Dolores Cannon, all people who have dared to go where no person has dared to go to before.

They are the ones who have broken down the barriers by developing, though trial and error, amazing techniques to help people.

For myself, I have a great passion and dedication for this work. I believe in it and through my own learning and experience have developed a technique that is as advanced as it is life changing.

Because of *fear*, hypnotherapists will, I imagine, continue to receive condemnation from various non-believers, who consider this work should be left well alone.

Being fearful is recognised as one of the most powerful emotions known to humankind, and often it is the fear of the unknown. Fearmongering was rife throughout the centuries gone past, people were paralysed with dread, they would do anything to avoid punishment. Leaders of the church, royalty, and leaders of armies spent most of their time devising strategies that would sustain their power, making certain the people knew there would be extreme retribution if certain rules were not followed. All of these methods were engineered to dominate in order to achieve the desired outcome of supreme leadership.

Any past experiences, good or bad, sit undetected deep in our Subconscious, and they have a rightful place, because they are a rich and necessary part of our growth. Nevertheless, to know we have an opportunity to understand these experiences for what they are, to expose them to the sunlight, can provide the perfect environment in which to appreciate the voyages our Souls have journeyed on. The voyages over the ebb and flow of this now vibrant, constantly changing world that encompasses our existence, wherever that may be. To have happiness and fulfilment is not for the select few, they are entitlements we are all meant to experience.

Yet how many of us find the time to understand what it takes to be happy and at peace ?

For first we must believe we are worthy.

So many clients have come to me with such terrible self-images, with burdens of guilt and shame weighing them down and holding them back from being loved by anyone, especially themselves.

Most of these people have addictions, the whole sorry mess goes hand in hand. Hypnotherapy reveals facets of ourselves that are enlightening, bringing to the surface an awareness, freedom, confidence and, most of all, a sense of wonder over who we are.

When something happens to us, we remember it and we learn a particular behaviour in response to what happened. Each time something similar happens, our physical and emotional reactions attached to the memory are repeated, and sometimes these reactions are unhealthy. With the support of hypnotherapy, the Subconscious somehow knows to take us to events in past lives that have led to current anxieties and concerns. It's a revelation to realise that when the conscious/ego mind is calm, the Subconscious mind can play such an important role in bringing together a clearer understanding of who we are.

Everybody will experience something different during a past life regression, and I encourage you not to feel apprehensive when I begin to investigate the questions you seek answers to, answers that will throw a light on your unique concerns. When we are sufficiently drained of external influences, then we can begin to heal and love ourselves.

I believe that guilt is the greatest of all human burdens and it can make us very sick. It can also cause many people to do some outrageous things. Seemingly happy-go-lucky people can be sucked into a vortex of emotional turmoil, sometimes leading to the ultimate act of suicide.

To reach this emotional state is horrific, and sadly it can be difficult to recognise. Fear goes hand in hand with all of this because somewhere along the human path those people have lost all sense of love for their self.

Over time we find ourselves building up thicker layers of skin to help get us through those difficult times, and sadly these layers cast a shadow over our true beautiful selves.

Hurt, shame, blame and judgements have blocked our natural progression to the point that overcoming these emotions is taking more and more courage, and it requires a very strong belief in our individual worth. To end the torment we must learn to listen to our inner self with compassion, and to stop judging and demoralising ourselves and know that there is always a Divine teacher within ready to help strengthen our resolve. By searching for answers externally, we do ourselves a great disservice, because there are lessons to be learned through life experiences that can only be learned through facing whatever stands in our way. We could end up missing the next step on our Soul's journey. When we are by ourselves in the shadows of our thoughts, we can create all kinds of scenarios for things that are not going our way.

Margaret was a perfect example of this, and she came to see me because she had been trying to fall pregnant for over a year. All sorts of things were happening to her body, she blamed herself and believed it was something she had done wrong. We sought the wisdom of her Subconscious, an experience that proved to be essential for understanding her situation.

I completely understand that a client's health, both physical and mental, is important, and when they express their concerns to me I know they are likely to be at their most vulnerable. So I feel it is important to listen with due care and responsibility to anyone looking for answers. To be understanding and compassionate, yet ready to refer them back to the care of their physician for any proper decision making on issues that require the delivery of respectful and appropriate healthcare.

Margaret settled into her regression well and before long she was experiencing a past life. She was standing on the edge of a clearing, deep in the forest, wearing nothing but a woven skirt which sat low beneath a huge belly. She watched on as men, women and children gathered about a fire in a large circle. She listened as shouts of laughter filled the air and to the sounds of the grass skirts worn by the women as they swished back and forth. I asked why she was not dancing.

"My belly is full of babies," she replied.

"How do you know there is more than one baby?"

"I just know."

Margaret described the dwelling she lived in. It was made from sticks from the forest floor and the roof was protected as it penetrated into overhanging dense foliage. Inside there was little else other than a grass pad for sleeping on. We moved forward to the time she was in labour, and there appeared to be an elderly woman, perhaps a midwife, to help things along.

Margaret could see that the young woman was having extreme difficulties, there was a lot of pain and not long after the birth of three babies, the young woman passed away. I gently encouraged her past the obvious traumatic emotions she'd felt when observing that moment, and I asked what purpose and lessons were there to be learned.

In the Light, the Soul of that beautiful girl felt sadness for not being able to be with her children. She also learned that death does not separate the love of one Soul for another, the purpose of that life was to teach her husband the value of trust and love. When she had accomplished that, her contract was complete and it was time to go home to the Light.

After connecting with the Subconscious, I asked for the reason why Margaret was shown that difficult life. It was to understand that in this lifetime she must learn patience and to lose the need to control every situation.

She also discovered that her husband in that lifetime was the one she is married to now, and that one of those triplets is their son Caleb.

The Subconscious told her not to fret, that the symptoms she had been experiencing, 'phantom feelings of pregnancy', was causing her to worry unduly about having more babies. It went on to explain that when she let go of her expectations and trusted herself instead of feeling unworthy and not capable, then Mother Nature would take its course.

I asked if there would there be more babies for Margaret. Yes, came the response, there will be two more for Margaret and they will be the Souls from that lifetime. Margaret did not need any convincing after that experience, as she saw for herself that time does not weaken the link between the love of the Soul family. She realised that her guilt at not falling pregnant was not due to any physical issue but to the undue pressure and expectations she had put upon herself. Many people load expectations on their shoulders until they become heavy burdens, the result usually showing up as heart problems, sore backs, and hip and knee issues and the like. We are not meant to suffer. The natural course of our life is meant to flow as a living energy, but when we build negative vibrations, it makes it harder to follow that course. As my Guides have said to me over the years, getting back to the basic foundations of trust, faith and love will create all the peace and harmony required for a contented life.

Chapter 33
When Lives Collide

We always see our worst selves. Our most vulnerable selves.
We need someone else to get close enough
to tell us we're wrong. Someone we trust.
David Levithan

Love and forgiveness are powerful anchors, and there usually comes a time in life when a window of opportunity opens, allowing us to grab hold of that anchor with both hands.

Time and time again I have had the honour of being trusted by many wonderful people, and have listened to complex issues, issues that have torn families apart. Misunderstandings, drugs, sex, crime, hate, judgement, religion, money, selfishness, pride, cruelty, greed and jealousy. These actions and feelings are generally the sum of all root causes of disenchantment. They are the crushing downside creating bitterness and mistrust, they are emotions that can manifest as mental illness or crippling pain. The Soul is not meant to suffer like this but it is what happens when we cannot change the pattern of our thoughts. We need to learn to forgive, and learn to let go.

Where there is love, there is healing, and when it flows freely out from a person, that energy radiates outwards in ever-increasing circles.

Wealth and power is by no means a form of protection, as nobody is impervious to facing difficulties and challenges.

We have to want to be healed, not just of illness but from fear and guilt.

You arrive into a new life full of zeal and strength, ready to learn from the mistakes you may have made in a previous life. You've probably heard the question 'why does it always happen to me?' Well there is a good reason it happens, because it is the strongest message you'll receive about what you are meant to learn.

Lessons repeat themselves over and over until you get it and if you do not get it, they become harder and harder, lifetime after lifetime until you learn. You are here in this lifetime to grow, and to help you along the journey there are individuals who will appear on your path to provide the very best chance for that growth to occur. You may also be there to help these individuals in return.

The true account I am about to relate was uncovered through a discussion with the Subconscious. It is, in part, about a person whose actions resulted in a terminal illness.

Stella had contacted me seeking answers, and she lived in Cairns, some 2000 kilometres away. But as so often happens, the Angels must have arranged it, because for other reasons I was travelling to Cairns the following week.

The special moments in my work are when I am getting to know someone and I realise something from the past is going to unlock a chain of events that will bring about a greater understanding. Meeting Stella for the first time brought those feelings to the surface immediately. I knew intuitively that this was going to occur. Stella's story is not that unusual, but the powerful message behind it became my reason to include it in this book.

This is Stella's story. Stella met Joe at a party, and straight-away she was drawn to his charismatic personality. Soon after they were dating regularly, eventually falling deeply love. Joe seemed to have everything Stella had ever dreamed of; he was loving, considerate, trustworthy, chivalrous and warm-hearted. Stella went on to tell me that a year later Joe proposed to her and she accepted believing they were to have a wonderful life together forever.

A wedding is one of the most exciting and memorable experiences of a person's life and the day was everything Stella could have hoped for. She described her beautiful wedding gown, the divine flowers, and she told me she had drawn many compliments that day as she wandered among the guests thinking in her mind that it was the happiest day of her life. Her dreams had come true, she had a handsome husband, wonderful family and friends, and there was lots of laughter and dancing into the night.

You might say everything was as perfect as it could possibly be. What she did not know was that Joe was watching everything with a different pair of eyes.

The very next day the abuse started, physical and mental. The shock was so great for Stella that she took it to mean Joe was simply overwhelmed by the whole wedding event. Sadly, this abuse lasted for years and years, and even after having children, they would be made to watch, as she endured mental abuse and horrific beatings, usually without a murmur from her lips.

Joe would be outraged that his powerful punches would not draw anything more than a whimper. But Stella did not want her children to be traumatised any more than they already were, nor did she want her extended family to be worried.

Stella could barely continue speaking about this horrific life she'd had.

I made a note that she'd divorced this man many years earlier, but it was no surprise to me that she was still handicapped by the trauma of it all, as were her adult children.

That day the Subconscious showed Stella three lives where the same Soul, 'Joe', had abused her over and over, but this lifetime was to be his last opportunity to make good. In spirit, they made a contract, one that would be broken if Joe could not mend his ways.

As you will soon discover, the sharing of experiences are not always what they seem, there is usually a measure of learning for both parties.

For Stella, it would be to stand up for herself, to recognise her worth and move on.

For Joe? Well let's see what happens.

Fear causes us to do things we might never have believed we could do, and for some people the need to control overrides everything. There is a constant burning inside of them to feed on the vulnerability of others, to always look for ways to feel powerful.

The boot camp I speak of throughout this book is not meant as a negative, but instead to highlight the very reasons we come here to learn. We haven't been booted into a nether-land by a higher power to be punished either. Humanity has already mastered this ability to punish without any added inducement. It is all about the Soul's progression, and this is why a conversation with the Subconscious is of such great value. It helps to unravel the complex webs we have woven, and bring about a *knowing* that empowers us to live on with faith and trust. We understand that we are worthy of our place in society, and most of all, we know we are loved.

Joe's lesson for this lifetime was to learn to let go of his own fears and the need to control. Unknown to his conscious awareness, Joe was repeating the same tragic mistakes, day after day as he continued to fill himself with vengeful thoughts. What he didn't realise was that he had made a second contract, one he had decided on so willingly before coming to Earth.

The Subconscious told Stella that Joe came back this time to be the best he could be, but that in the event he could not fulfil this contract, he had put down for himself a lesson, a second contract, that would teach him unconditional love, a lesson that would show him how important the kindness and care from others was to his needs.

So, she had agreed to give him one more chance.

Unfortunately for Joe, the second contract, a binding agreement, was waiting in the wings ready for a swift and immediate action. There are no excuses left.

One of the most alarming things to experience when we cannot look after ourselves is relying on someone else. Anyone suffering in this way will tell you that the feeling of powerlessness can be humiliating and debilitating. Being unable to control your own life, knowing there is no way out other than to go forward is something one would have no choice about.

Long after Stella had divorced Joe, he contacted her one day to say he was unwell. He had moments of lethargy, his appetite was gone and his back ached so badly that he'd begun staying in bed longer and longer each day. She recommended that he should go for medical help, but this was a most unfavourable suggestion and he said as much. But within a few weeks the body was screaming out, and he had no choice. After many exhaustive tests, Joe was diagnosed with spine cancer, and almost at the speed of light he lost the ability to walk and care for himself. The treatments were rugged and took a huge toll on him physically and mentally. Worse was to come. He had to go into a nursing home to be cared for.

No longer could he go to the bathroom on his own, nor feed himself, and his eyesight was worsening to the point where he relied entirely on 24-hour care. He was now relying on the love and devotion of the dedicated doctors and nurses, but they alone could not provide the cure for the ache in Joe's heart. He needed family love.

The Subconscious, that higher part of her true self, was so gentle in its advice to Stella. It explained that the fear of guilt for not reaching out to Joe was also making her ill. It went on to explain that the experience Joe was having was for his higher good, that he had asked for this lesson and no matter how difficult it may appear, in the fullness of time his Soul would be grateful for having mastered the understanding of unconditional love and non-judgement.

The Subconscious spoke to Stella and told her to have a time of reflection, and that Joe's journey was not her own. She left that day with what I believe was a real understanding, particularly knowing none of it was her fault.

Joe is in the latter stages of dementia now, a cursory relief from the cancer, his time on this plane will soon be over.

He has had to learn in the hardest of ways and obviously, like all hindsight thoughts, he will have reflected often on his actions.

Even though Joe lost his way, his Soul will be mighty grateful for the lesson learned.

All paths lead in the same direction to learning, the only difference for each of us is that we may take a little longer to get there.

Throughout the year I've been writing this book, I have become more and more aware of how unique our individual journeys are. The only regret I have is in not being able to write everybody's story. Connecting to each individual Subconscious has been a phenomenal and awe-inspiring education.

What I have taken from those conversations is that there is a power far greater than ourselves, whether we wish to acknowledge that or not, is another matter entirely.

I will be the first one to admit that we will never know until we die what actually happens to our Soul; having said that, I do not have one shred of doubt that the wisdom and knowledge shared by the many Subconscious minds I have spoken to is nothing but the truth.

If by writing this book I have been able to influence your thinking about the importance of believing in goodness, of treating others with kindness and compassion, of understanding that we are here to learn from each other, that the whole matter of life on Earth is about gratitude and appreciation, then I will feel as though I have accomplished what I set out to do.

Do not allow fear and guilt to steer you away from your spiritual path. Instead, embrace life, let go of the things you cannot change, forgive yourself, forgive your opponents, reflect back on the stories I have shared and realise how important it is to be the change. The change that brings about peace on our Earth.

Humanity has survived thousands of years of growth, through good, bad and difficult times and we have inflicted reprehensible acts of cruelty upon each other, almost as if our greatest wish is to self-destruct. But we cannot escape fate nor avoid the consequences that may inhibit us; after all it is the journey of the Soul that is in progress.

Our battle is always with the self.

I love that there are like-minded people who are collectively working towards peace, uninhibited by naysayers, no longer fearful of persecution as they may have been in the past.

At a time when technology is a part of our daily ritual, let us not forget our true purpose on Earth and make the journey we took to the toughest planet in the Universe as painless as possible.

It is your God-given right to be loved, so as you traverse from one lifetime to the next, through all boundaries of time and space, be comforted that your Soul is loved, protected and immortal.

About the Author

Elizabeth Taylor-Wey Dip. PLRT

ELIZABETH TAYLOR HAS HER private practice in Queensland, Australia.

She developed the Advance Past Life Regression Hypnotherapy technique, a course approved by the International Institute for Complementary Therapists, for the benefit of humankind. She is an accredited training provider and is revered by those who have learned under her mentoring.

An expert communicator, Elizabeth's skills have been enhanced by decades of spiritual discovery and personal experience, and she uses these experiences to lift the spirits of people by changing their attitudes, and by helping them to validate their worth. She also offers seminars in which the audience members get to have some amazing Spiritual experiences. If you would like more information about Elizabeth's courses or her other work, please visit www.elizabethtaylor.com.au.

E-mail: elizabethtaylor585@gmail.com

Follow Elizabeth on Facebook: www.facebook.com/elizabeth.taylor

Resource Guide

Helena Lancaster
Certified Clairvoyant Healer
Advanced Past Life Regression Hypnotherapist Level Two
Full Professional Member IICT
e: helena@abundanthealingwisdom.com
w: abundanthealingwisdom.com

Neil Davidson
e: neilakos35@hotmail.co.uk
Certified Healing Touch Practitioner (Level 4)
Certified Past Life Regression Facilitator (Advanced Level, Toni Reilly Institute)

Victoria White
Astrologer
Advance Past Life Regression Hypnotherapist Level Two
e: contact@queenofzeus.com

Donald James Waters OAM
Australian Contemporary Artist
Public Speaker
Art Therapy Educator Mentor

Sylvia Marson
Managing editor, eagle eye editing
e: sylvia@eagleeyeediting.com.au
www.eagleeyeediting.com.au

Donald James Waters OAM
Front Cover artist

I am honoured to have been approached by Elizabeth to design the front cover of her book. I have worked with many people using art as a therapy, learning to paint from the Subconscious. The art of teaching people to look inward and truly understand who they are and appreciation for the journey they are on is my passion.

The understandings that emotion can be clearly expressed through creative writing, colour, line, shape or pattern are an integral part of both my art and teaching. While my art deals with the present, Elizabeth has ventured deeper into the subconscious and determines what has been before in order to define who we are now. I believe the opportunity to look within yourself to understand the highs, lows and background that make up who you are at this point in time; you are gaining a confidence and strength to cope with everyday existence. My dealings with mental illness, low self-esteem, PTSD, suicide, self-harm among the general highs and lows of everyday life, show a clear sign of lack of self-confidence and hesitancy to communicate.

One of the concerns in exposing the past is that positives as well as negatives will appear as the driving force determining who we are at this point in time. Over the years I have been able to expose emotion and turn negatives into positives, thus enabling people to move forward with a clear direction.

DONALD JAMES WATERS IS an established Australian contemporary artist with an illustrious career spanning over three decades.

Donald's artworks have made their way into the catalogues of many private and corporate collectors worldwide, including that of her Majesty Queen Elizabeth II. Donald has involved himself in many community arts programs and completed government commissioned art projects. In 2016, Donald was awarded with an Order Of Australia Medal (OAM) for services to the community and the Arts. In 2010, he was recognised as Gold Coast Citizen of the Year. In addition to exhibiting in art galleries worldwide, Donald is available for commissioned artworks, art technique workshops, art therapy workshops, art lecturing and critiques, motivational speaking and hosting. For more information www.djwaters.com.au or contact don@djwtaers.com.au or +61 7 55461272. Please follow Donald James Waters on Facebook to keep up to date with his adventures. *www.facebook.com/DonaldJWaters.*

Printed in Australia
AUOC02n0828210217
283212AU00005B/5/P

9 781925 516777